NORTH ANYTOWN   BY OWNER
5BR House on Pond   Deck   Patio
Den w/fpl   Din Rm   Liv Rm   3 Baths
$99,500 or Best Reasonable Offer
Inspection Sat.–Sun. 10–5
House will be sold by Sunday Night to
Highest Bidder   (608) 555-3138

How to Sell Your Home in 5 Days

By William G. Effros

WORKMAN PUBLISHING, NEW YORK

**Library of Congress
Cataloging-in-Publication Data**
Effros, William G.
How to sell your home in 5 days
by William G. Effros.
p.   cm.
ISBN 1-56305-496-5
1. House Selling. I. Title.
HD1379.E35   1993
333.33'83—dc20   93-14445
CIP

Workman Publishing
708 Broadway
New York, New York 10003

Published in the United States of America
First printing September 1993
10 9 8 7 6 5 4 3 2 1

PUBLISHER'S NOTE

This book does not provide legal opinions or advice and does not substitute for the advice of counsel in assessing and minimizing legal risks in the sale of your home. Readers are directed to the chapter "Why You Need an Attorney" beginning at page 191. An attorney familiar with the laws affecting the sale of real estate in your state should be consulted before implementing the methods suggested.

CONTENTS

A TRUE STORY

The procedure for selling a home in 5 days is based on a true story. I developed it to sell my own home.

At first I was going to sell my home the conventional way. When I spoke to my real estate broker, he said: "Why don't you just hold on to it for another six months? The market has to be better by then."

Six months later, the market was worse.

When I spoke to my real estate broker again, he said: "Well, I suppose we could run a desperation sale and get rid of it."

So I thought to myself: Why do I need a broker to run a desperation sale? I can run a desperation sale all by myself! Besides, with no broker, I won't have to pay a 6% fee.

Let me try this, I thought. In figuring out how to run my own sale, I came up with the basis for my 5-Day Plan. If it didn't work, all I'd lose was 5 days of my time and a couple of hundred dollars. But if it did work, I'd save over $15,000 in brokerage fees.

So I placed an ad in the local newspapers.

I received more than 100 responses, and more than 40 prospective buyers came to visit my home during the 2 days it was open for inspection. There were a dozen serious bids. Six were higher than the asking price.

I made $32,790 more than I would have made if I'd sold my home through a broker.

THE 5-DAY PLAN

On Wednesday you run an ad like this in the classified section of your local newspapers:

> NORTH ANYTOWN   BY OWNER
> 5BR House on Pond   Deck   Patio
> Den w/fpl   Din Rm   Liv Rm   3 Baths
> $99,500 or Best Reasonable Offer
> Inspection Sat.–Sun. 10–5
> House will be sold by Sunday Night to
> Highest Bidder   (608) 555-3138

By Sunday night your home will be sold for the best possible price.

You will sell your home in 5 days.

Really.

And, if you play your cards right, you could even enjoy the process.

This book explains how the process works, why it works, and what you must do to make it work for you. The simple ad shown above is the key to selling your home in 5 days. If you follow the plan outlined in this book, and modify it to fit your own style, you will sell your home in 5 days and receive the highest possible price.

A QUICK COURSE IN MARKETING

The Free Enterprise System

This section is included to acquaint you with the theoretical underpinnings of the 5-Day Plan so you'll understand that the success of this technique is not some once-in-a-lifetime fluke, like winning the lottery.

The 5-Day Plan for selling homes is based on the classical free-enterprise economic model. In *Wealth of Nations* Adam Smith (the 18th-century economist from Scotland, not the guy on public television) introduced the concepts of "perfect competition" and an "invisible hand." Essentially, what Smith said was that perfect competition exists when no individual can control the market; instead, an invisible hand controls the market to provide the maximum benefit to everyone in society.

As it happens, the housing market in the United States is about as close as any market gets to perfect competition. There are too many individual buyers and sellers for anyone to control the market. There are no monopolies or oligopolies. There are always some buyers. The market is free to rise and fall according to the rules of supply and demand.

If you offer your home for sale, describe it accurately and disclose everything that's wrong with it, an invisible hand will assign it a fair market price. This is the characteristic trait of perfect competition. It protects both buyers and sellers. It works whether you understand it or not. It works every time a home changes ownership.

Homes invariably sell at their fair market price.

THE GREATER FOOL THEORY

The 1980s were sustained by an economic concept known as the Greater Fool Theory. The main tenet of this theory was that you didn't have to worry about foolishly paying too much for something, because no matter how foolish you were, a greater fool would come along to bail you out by paying more than you did.

This theory fueled the rise in the stock market, the money market, the junk-bond market and the housing market.

In the housing market, banks and savings-and-loan institutions contributed to the Greater Fool Theory by providing mortgage money to any fool who came along to buy any home that came along at any price. The banks and S&Ls didn't have to worry about the prices paid because, ultimately, their loans were guaranteed by the federal government.

Those days are over. The Greater Fool Theory won't work anymore. Today you can be quite sure no greater fool will come along to bail you out of your mistakes.

The free ride is also over for the banks and the S&Ls. If anything, these institutions are less likely than ever to lend money unless they're positive the value of the home will never go below what the buyers are willing to pay for it.

Buyers today can afford to pay only what they're sure a home is worth. Most of the speculators are gone. Everyone is fearful of becoming the greatest fool, the one who winds up owning a home for a price much higher than anyone else will pay.

When in doubt, today's buyers will pass up any home they feel might be priced too high.

Inflation and Deflation

We are accustomed to living in inflationary times. We almost expect the cost of things to go up from one year to the next. This situation has existed since the end of the 1940s.

During the 1970s, inflation really got out of hand. There were some years when the cost of things increased by more than 10% from one year to the next. People sold their used cars for more than they paid for them when they were new.

Discussions of inflation became part of our daily conversation. We spoke of "sticker shock" when we first noticed that our cars cost more than our parents spent for their homes. We moaned about the demise of "penny candy" and laughed about what things now cost in "five-and-ten-cent" stores.

But we never complained about the fact that the most valuable thing we own, our homes, also skyrocketed in price during these times. Homes our parents and grandparents bought for $10,000 in the 1950s were worth $25,000 by the mid-1970s, $50,000 by the early 1980s, $100,000 by the mid-1980s.

Thanks to inflation, home owners made a lot of money on their homes in the 1980s.

Then came the 1987 stock market crash. Stocks dropped 20% in value in one day, and the real estate market followed. Homes dropped 20% to 25%

in value. Inflation is under control now, and that's good. But the value of our homes has not recovered and is increasing by only 1% to 2% a year—if at all. Some homes are still decreasing in value.

The drop in real estate values that accompanied the stock market crash defines the word "deflation." The real estate did not change, but its value was suddenly deflated. Many buyers who purchased their homes just before the '87 stock market crash discovered that, overnight, their homes were worth less than they owed the bank. Some simply moved out of their homes and sent the bank the keys, creating a glut of homes for sale that further deflated prices.

Most of us had never seen deflation before. We'd become adjusted to inflation by buying things and profiting when their value increased. Now, for the first time, we've seen that things can go down in value, too.

THE BUYERS

THE BUYER POOL

At any given time, only a certain number of buyers will be interested in a home like yours in a location like yours at a price like yours. This group of buyers is called the "buyer pool" for your home. The participants constantly change as some buyers purchase homes, or get frustrated and leave the pool, while others decide to buy and enter the pool.

Many sellers make the mistake of restricting the size of their buyer pool by pricing their homes too high. They expect to be offered less than the asking price, so they raise the price to get a higher bid.

Few home buyers are experienced. Most are dimly aware that some home sellers may accept less than the asking price, but they don't know how much less. They see a certain price and say, "We can't afford that—let's not even bother to look." When this happens, the seller has decreased the size of the buyer pool. Some buyers who shut themselves out of the pool may have been prepared to offer more than the amount finally accepted, but the seller will never know. This results in a lower selling price for the home.

When you use the 5-Day Plan, you offer your home for less than you think you'll actually get in order to attract more buyers, who will bid against one another for the privilege of buying your home. *This results in a higher selling price for your home.*

But what if your home is an oddball? What if it's so far off the beaten path that you despair of anyone ever finding it? Maybe your home is in bad shape or is located next to a chemical dump. What if you can't imagine that anyone would want your home?

You bought your home. You overlooked some things and made allowances for others. For some reason your home was attractive to you. And at a certain price it will be attractive to other people. Your job is to make sure the people who would find your home attractive know it's for sale at a price they're willing to pay.

The 5-Day Plan allows you to make a big splash in the buyer pool. You must make sure your ad is seen by virtually everyone actively looking for a home like yours. If enough buyers respond, you will sell your home, in 5 days, for the highest possible price.

THE SELLERS' MARKET

During most of the 1980s we experienced a "sellers' market" for homes. There were fewer home sellers than home buyers. In this situation anyone who owned a home could make money.

There were waiting lists for new homes. Builders were paid for homes before they were started. In some places the value of existing homes doubled each year. Speculators bought two or three homes, held them for six months, and then sold them for much more than they had paid.

Home sellers knew that if they didn't get their asking price, all they had to do was wait and the value of their homes would rise.

If you owned a home, you couldn't lose.

But those days are gone. They ended in 1987 with the stock market crash, the S&L crisis, and the beginning of the prolonged recession. So many people lost so much money that it will be a long time before we see another sellers' market for homes.

Many of those who bought homes just before the market crashed have discovered that they can no longer get back what they paid. A home purchased for $100,000 in August 1987 was worth only $75,000 by the end of the year. With inflation pushing up prices at just 1% to 2% a year, that home won't be worth $100,000 again until after the year 2000.

The price of the average home dropped by 25% or more in most regions of the country. Home owners who wait to sell their homes will pay more in interest than they will gain from inflation. Their net worth will decline with every passing month. The longer they wait, the worse it will get.

The sellers' market is gone, and it won't be back for a long, long time. In today's market, the faster you can sell your home, the more money you'll put in your pocket for future investment or retirement.

There is no faster way to sell your home than the 5-Day Plan.

THE BUYERS' MARKET

If the 1980s market was accurately referred to as a "sellers' market," then today's market can fairly be called a "buyers' market." Plenty of homes are still being bought and sold, but now there are fewer buyers than sellers. This situation leaves buyers in the stronger negotiating position. Buyers can shop around for the best deal.

Buyers generally inspect a number of homes before making up their minds. They get a good sense of what homes cost and compare one home with others like it to decide what it's worth. They are under no pressure to bid more than they think a home is worth for fear that some other buyer will come along and offer more.

Fewer buyers will look at homes priced too high. Of those buyers, none will offer the asking price. Eventually the seller will either take less or fail to sell the home.

The buyers' market is of no concern to you if you use the 5-Day Plan. This method will work in a buyers' or sellers' market. It will work in inflationary or deflationary times. It will work during booms and busts.

By using the 5-Day Plan, you position your home as the best deal on the market and the next home to be sold. Buyers for a home like yours must come to look at it—right away. It will be sold by Sunday night to the highest bidder.

For this 5-day period your home is the best deal on the market and serious buyers *will* come to take a look.

The important thing to remember is that while many homes are still being bought and sold, some will go on the market and fail to sell. If you use the 5-Day Plan, your home will be one of those sold and you'll get the most money possible.

THE BROKER
DEBATE

ARE BROKERS WORTH IT?

Don't get me wrong. I have nothing against real estate brokers. Some of my best friends are brokers. They helped me buy and sell many homes.

Twenty-five years ago, my wife and I bought a five-bedroom stone house in Philadelphia for $7,500. Our broker found the house, checked it out, showed us what was wrong with it, helped us negotiate the price and arranged for us to pick up the existing 4% mortgage.

Our broker was a family friend. We didn't really find her; she found us. We weren't even thinking of buying a home when she suggested we consider this one. She was enormously competent, had been in the business for 15 years and was a principal in her firm. She worked hard for her money and made our dealings with her a total success.

The brokerage fee on our first home was 6%, or $450. The seller paid the fee. It was a great deal.

Times have changed. The last home we sold was a five-bedroom colonial in Stamford, Connecticut, which we planned to offer for only $255,000 in a "desperation sale." When we realized that at 6% the brokerage fee would be $15,300, we started looking for another way to sell.

Now, we understand that the cost of living has escalated for real estate brokers as well as everyone else, and that a fee of $450 might be a little on the low side today. However, allowing for the same cost-of-living increase that everyone else got, $450 would be worth about $1,500 today, which sounds about right. A fee of $15,300 seems a bit steep for conducting a desperation sale.

Along with many other people, we harbor serious doubts that real estate brokers today are worth what they're paid.

WHO ARE THESE PEOPLE?

In the 1960s I ran a school for real estate brokers in Camden, New Jersey. I was just out of college and knew nothing about real estate, but that didn't matter. My job was simply to round up people for the class, take their money and pay the instructors who presented the material.

The class was a cram course. It taught prospective brokers a layman's version of the law as applied to the purchase and sale of homes through licensed brokers. It did not attempt to sort out people with good business sense from people with no sense at all. It met state requirements. We guaranteed passage of the state test. In 15 weeks we took people, some dumber than hockey pucks, and turned them into state-licensed real estate brokers.

The majority of real estate brokers have little more experience in selling homes than you do. Many are part-timers who hope they'll be in the right place at the right time to stumble onto a huge commission. Many entered the field during the '80s, when selling homes was no more difficult than falling into a ditch.

Brokers receive no training in how to price homes. That is left to local knowledge and common sense. You have no way to evaluate how much common sense your broker has. Most brokers will try a high price and see if anyone buys; if not, they'll keep dropping the price until somebody comes along who will pay it. Once brokers sign you to an exclusive contract, it's of no great concern to them if your home remains unsold for a year because the asking price is out of range. You're locked in for the entire period of the contract, and there is nothing you can do about it.

On the other hand, what if your home sells immediately? Maybe that's worse. Maybe you sold too cheaply and could have gotten much more. You'll never know.

Your home is probably your most valuable asset. Selling it for the right amount is the best way to protect your financial future. If you do it yourself, using the 5-Day Plan, you can rest assured it will be done properly.

It doesn't take a lot to become a real estate broker.

Beware false expertise.

CHOOSING A BROKER

You don't need a real estate broker every day, or even every year; you may not need one every decade. It is unlikely that you have a regular real estate broker.

On what basis, then, should you choose an agent to conduct one of the most important financial transactions of your life?

Most brokers are selected on the basis of personal recommendations. This doesn't make much sense because your friends and relatives often have no more basis for making a selection than you do. But they want to be helpful, so they wind up recommending someone they know who is "in the business."

Many people are in the real estate business because it's possible to make staggering sums of money while expending minimal effort. What's more, it's relatively simple to become a licensed real estate broker. So lots of people try. In my town, for example, there is one licensed real estate broker for every 10 homes.

So how to choose?

You end up closing your eyes, picking a name and hoping for the best.

This a strange way to make such an important decision. Nonetheless, it's the approach used by most people.

THE PRICING BAIT AND SWITCH

If you're shopping around for a broker to sell your home for you, watch out for the pricing bait and switch.

Brokers present themselves as having more experience than you when it comes to pricing homes. They know you have little or no experience either in choosing a broker or in pricing a home. To make sure you select them to represent you exclusively, they tell you what you want to hear about the price for your home.

"Wow," you say, "this broker will get me more money for my home than anyone else. This is the broker for me!"

This is a sure prescription for disaster. After your home has been on the market for three months, or six or nine months, and nobody has come to see it (with the possible exception of the broker's cousin), one of you will suggest dropping the price.

By now, you're desperate. Your home has become a lead weight around your neck. You've got to get rid of it. Fast! You no longer care what you get for it, as long as you can put an end to the monthly payments. Just stopping the pain will feel good.

So you drop the price. Buyers realize that your home has been on the market for months and that you're in trouble. Other brokers steer their clients to you because you're selling cheap. You're offered even less than you're now asking. But it's the first offer you've received. You want to sell before the price goes down even further. You have no choice. You sell.

Adding insult, and some more injury, to injury—you still have to pay the brokerage commission. The broker who got you into all this trouble still makes out like a bandit!

I can't tell you how to select a broker, but I can tell you how *not* to select one. Stay away from brokers who talk about impossible prices if you sign exclusive deals with them.

Don't fall for the pricing bait and switch.

WHO DOES THE BROKER WORK FOR?

When you hire someone, it's appropriate to assume that this person will work in your interest. In real estate transactions this is not the case.

If you sell your home the conventional way, you're represented by a real estate broker, and in most instances a different broker will represent the buyer. The "buyer's broker" is not paid by the buyer. The buyer usually pays no fee at all. The seller normally pays the fee for both the "buyer's broker" and the "seller's broker."

In this situation, whose interests does the "buyer's broker" represent? If the broker's entire fee is being paid by the seller, it's fairly obvious that no one truly represents the buyer's interests in the transaction. This problem has become so clear that some states have passed laws requiring brokers to remind buyers that no one in the deal is being paid to represent them.

But you are the seller. It is not your problem if buyers don't know that you pay all commission fees. Your problem is that the broker gets no fee if there is no deal. A bad deal for the seller is better for the broker than no deal at all. So brokers may try to push sellers into accepting deals that are not in the seller's best interest. (Even if the seller subsequently backs out of a bad deal, the broker still gets paid!)

Compounding this problem is the practice of real estate brokers who buy homes directly from sellers to add to their own inventory, provided they can persuade the owners to sell for a low enough price. Do you think the real estate broker can possibly represent the seller's best interest when the broker is also the buyer? Often the real estate broker will take another 6% out of the sale price by charging the seller both the "buyer's broker" and "seller's broker" commissions.

If you sell your home the conventional way, it's important to understand that the broker does not primarily represent your interests. Because the broker's fee is paid only on a contingency basis, the broker really represents only the broker.

WORSE, NOT BETTER

You may think that working with a broker will ease the emotional stress of selling your home. Nothing could be farther from the truth.

Your broker may feel an obligation to be absolutely brutal with you about the way you've painted or decorated your home. Your broker may suggest that you change things you happen to love. If you decide to sell through a broker instead of using the 5-Day Plan, you will certainly stretch the selling period and its attendant pain.

Most brokers will demand an exclusive contract for at least six months. Many will insist on a minimum of nine months or a year. Because of the way they sell homes, brokers know that it will take between six months and a year. During this time you are locked in to your broker. If the broker is doing little or nothing for you, all you can do is wait for the contract period to come to an end. If you sell the home yourself, the broker still gets a commission.

Every time you enter your home, the lockbox your broker affixed to your door will remind you that you've put it up for sale. When you see the lockbox, you'll begin to wonder whether anyone else has been in your home since the last time you were there.

If you're planning to sell your home the conventional way, be prepared to keep your home spotless *for a year or more*! There's no telling when someone will want to come see it. You can't afford to put off anyone who might turn out to be the buyer.

You must be prepared to vacate your home at a moment's notice when any broker wants to bring potential buyers. Brokers don't want you around. They may want to say things to prospective buyers that would make you angry. They may think your taste is atrocious or laughable. They may even want to suggest that the buyer destroy things that are precious to you.

Once you've signed with a broker, you won't be able to back out of the contract for a long time. If the broker brings you a buyer who agrees to your terms, you are obligated to pay the broker's commission whether or not you consummate the deal.

Think long and hard before signing up with a broker.

THE 5-DAY ADVANTAGE

A GOOD DEAL FOR EVERYONE

The 5-Day Plan works because it's a good deal for everyone.

The seller knows exactly when the home will be sold and can offer it at the most convenient time. The buyer looks at a home that's ready for immediate occupancy.

The inspection period is short (just 2 days) and selected by the seller. The seller's household is not continually jarred out of its routine by unexpected visits from brokers bringing unscheduled potential buyers. Sellers who use the 5-Day Plan are ready to receive buyers who feel welcome and unhurried as they inspect the home. Buyers can stay as long as they like. Those who come on Saturday can come back again on Sunday with friends and advisers.

The seller can consider lower bids than would be acceptable using a more conventional approach. A good rule of thumb is to ask a price 10% under the price of similar homes sold through a broker. Even if the home is actually sold for this price, the seller will probably net at least as much money as if a broker had conducted the sale.

Few homes in a buyers' market sell for the listed price. Conventional sellers can expect offers from 5% to as much as 50% under the asking price. If they accept one of these bids, they'll be giving at least a 5% discount coupled with at least a 6% brokerage fee.

However, the 5-Day Plan does not depend on selling at a discount and saving the broker's commission. These are just factors that provide an extra measure of safety and profit. If the sale is conducted properly, the home will sell for as much as, or more than, the selling price of the same home offered by a broker.

Because the initial asking price is lower than it would be if a broker conducted the sale, there are a greater number of potential buyers. With more interested parties, the home may sell for more than the asking price. Buyers know that even if they offer more than the asking price, they're still getting a very good deal. They know there are half a dozen other potential buyers willing to pay within $500 of the final price. They know they have not made a foolish bid.

The home may sell for less than the asking price, or it may sell for more than the asking price. In either case, both the buyer and the seller can be sure that the 5-Day Plan resulted in the best possible deal *for both of them.*

MAKE MORE MONEY

Stop dreaming about some rich fool coming along and offering you more than you know your home is worth. It won't happen.

There are more homes on the market than there are buyers. Buyers know this. They know sellers are settling for less than the asking price. They know some sellers are getting no bids at all. They know many sellers are desperate. They know some sellers will be stuck with their homes or forced to sell them for less than their market value. They know that each home sold for less than market value puts additional pressure on other home sellers to lower their prices.

The 5-Day Plan takes you out of this loop.

You do not sit beside your telephone, day after day, praying that a real estate broker will bring a potential buyer to see your home. You do not ask some ridiculously high price and wait for a counteroffer. You tell all available buyers that you will allow *them* to establish a fair market price for your home. Because no brokers are involved, you can afford to sell your home for less, and you're prepared to do so in return for a quick sale.

Buyers understand what you're doing as soon as they see your ad. They know your home is the best deal on the market and you can afford to accept 10% less for your home than you could if you sold it conventionally. They will compete with each other for your home. They would all like to take advantage of this 10% discount. They would love to get an even larger discount, but they're not fools. A 9% discount is still a good deal. So is an 8% discount. Or a 7% discount.

The whole notion of discounts implies that there is some kind of list price. But, of course, there isn't. When knowledgeable buyers are surrounded by other knowledgeable buyers who feel your home is worth more than you're asking, they may bid it up over the price you think it's worth. If the bid fails to reach the asking price, you didn't price your home properly, and it's silly to think a broker will bring you a buyer who will pay 10% over a price that no one would bid.

No matter how much you finally get for your home, you will keep more money if you use the 5-Day Plan than if you sell your home using the conventional approach.

SELL FASTER

Nobody talks about selling your home for you in 5 days. Nobody! But *you* will sell your home in 5 days if you use this method.

- In 5 days you will locate and show your home to virtually all currently active buyers in the buyer pool.

- You will spare your family the ordeal of a lengthy period of stress while your home is on the market.

- You will not have all kinds of people inspecting your home at all hours for what seems an eternity.

- You will not get desperate.

You will make up your mind to sell your home. You will put it on the market. You will work very hard for 5 days. You will sell your home.

In 5 days it's all over.

PICK THE TIME

Putting a home on the market the conventional way is a nerve-racking affair. If you've never done it, be thankful for what the 5-Day Plan will spare you.

In a conventional sale, you know you'll move but you don't know when. You may have to buy a new home before you've sold the old one, or you may have to get out of your old home before you've found a new one. You never know when a buyer might come by, so your old home must be in spotless condition at all times. You have to keep valuable belongings hidden because potential buyers sometimes turn out to be thieves evaluating your home as a possible target.

It isn't fun, and it can go on for a year or more. Your life is on hold while you wait.

When we planned to move from Pennsylvania to New York in 1972, my wife and I decided to build our new home. After the frame was up, and things seemed to be going along fine, we put our Philadelphia home on the market. Our new home was scheduled to be finished in January 1973, two months away, and we figured it was impossible to complete the sale in less time than that. We were wrong. Within a week we had buyers for our old home. They wanted to take possession right away, but after tough negotiations they agreed to give us our two months.

That December a severe ice storm in Connecticut downed miles of electrical cable. All the cable on the East Coast was sent to Connecticut for use in the emergency, leaving none to attach our all-electric house in New York to the power grid. In January we moved into our almost completed home with no electricity and no heat. It was a horrendous winter. My wife was pregnant. Then came the gasoline crisis, and we couldn't get enough fuel for our portable generator.

We lived like that for three months. Cold. Mad. Struggling in our brand-new home with contractors still swarming all over the place. It was a nightmare. Twenty years later the bad taste still lingers. I vowed then that in the future I would always control the exact timing of the sale and purchase of my home.

The 5-Day Plan has allowed me to do that.

MAINTAIN COMPLETE CONTROL

When you sell your home through a broker, you relinquish control over many aspects of the sale.

You never know exactly what's happening because you have to rely on the broker for most of your information.

- The broker decides where and how often to advertise.

- The broker insists on putting a "lockbox" on your door so that any broker with a key to the box can get into your home at any time. The broker will also want to put an ungainly "For Sale" sign on your lawn, which may remain there for months or even years.

- Buyers contact brokers, not you, and a broker who doesn't happen to like you or your home can steer them toward other sellers.

- The broker may tell prospective buyers that you're having a hard time selling your home or that you're desperate. (A broker once told me, even before I indicated an interest in buying, "They're asking $600,000, but of course they'll take twenty-five percent less.")

- The broker gets a commission even if you find the buyer and make the sale.

When you sell your home using the 5-Day Plan, you retain complete control of the sale.

- You can price your home without regard to brokers' commissions or extra fees for extra advertising.

- You select the exact time of the sale.

- You prepare for the inspection and show your home at the best time for you.

- You don't have to disappear when buyers come to look at your home. Often you can immediately answer questions that brokers cannot answer. As you speak with potential buyers, you get a chance to sense if they're serious about buying your home.

- You get instant feedback on every aspect of your sale.

- You decide exactly what you are prepared to accept.

- You are under no obligation to accept an offer you don't like.

From start to finish, you are the one who takes charge of your sale.

AVOID RISK

There is no risk when you sell your home using the 5-Day Plan. After all, what's the worst that can happen?

Nobody calls. Nobody comes. You fail to sell your home.

But in just 5 days you know where you stand. If nobody calls, you can be sure your home isn't worth anything near what you asked. If it was worth a little less, somebody would have offered a little less. Even if you advertised in the wrong places, your home should still be the best deal on the market and somebody should have called.

At this point, you must review. Run down the checklist at the back of this book. Did you do everything right? Ask yourself if you still want to sell even if you can't get close to what you were hoping for. Maybe you'll decide the 5-Day Plan is just a bad idea.

But what have you lost?

There is nothing to stop you from selling your home the conventional way. Contact real estate brokers. Find out how much *they* think your home is worth. If they say they can get 10% more than you were asking, let them put it on the market. See how they do.

But if they come back to you after six months of failure and suggest you drop your price by 10% or 25%, think about trying the 5-Day Plan again. Go back onto the market with another ad at the right price and sell your home in 5 days.

ARE YOU REALLY READY?

This sounds like a rhetorical question, but it's not. The 5-Day Plan works so fast, it's almost over before it begins. The process is radically different from the conventional method. You must *really* be ready before you start this chain of events.

Traditionally, people who don't have to move start by saying they would sell their home if someone came along who offered them more money than they think it's worth. With sugarplums dancing in their heads, they locate a real estate broker and "list" their home at an inflated price. They haven't even begun to think seriously about moving, because no serious buyer would pay the price they're asking. People using this method are fully prepared to sit around for months, or years, knowing it's unlikely they will ever sell their home at the listed price.

The 5-Day Plan works the other way around. It unites a buyer who is ready to buy with a seller who is ready to sell. The buyer and seller work together to achieve their common goal. Everyone else is forced out of the middle until a final price is negotiated. Only then are professionals brought in to conclude the financial and legal aspects in the conventional way.

If you're really ready to sell, after reading and absorbing this book, you will spend a total of 5 days of very intense work. By the end of the 5 days, you will have located a buyer and sold your home.

If you're not really ready, don't start.

FIRST THINGS
FIRST

DECISIONS, DECISIONS

Because the 5-day sale happens very quickly, your mind must be clear from the outset and you must fully understand what you're doing at all times.

Be sure you're committed to the idea. You must know, and the people who come to see your home must believe, that you'll follow through.

- You must decide when to make new living arrangements and whether you'll show your home empty or full of your furniture.

- You must line up an attorney and discuss your plan.

- You must plan for a home inspection by a certified firm. If your state requires it, you must conduct a radon test. You must fix some things and not fix others. You must make your home look as good as it can look.

- You must price your home and decide the absolute lowest amount you will accept. Would you take less if it was the best you could get?

- You must decide how much advertising to place, and where to place it.

- You must write the rules for the sale. You must determine the bidding procedure.

- You must compile detailed information about your home for prospective buyers. You must set up a phone log.

- You must decide how to handle security.

All these decisions must be fixed in your mind.

Be sure you are comfortable with each step you take. Be sure you believe in what you are doing.

Do not proceed until you are.

Golden Rules

Remember that you determine the rules for this sale. Never lose sight of the fact that your home is *your* property and that *you* will decide exactly how to sell it. If you maintain control of the process, there is no risk involved in using this method.

Think through your position very carefully before the process gets under way. You are selling your home in an unconventional way, and you must understand what you're doing and how you're doing it well enough to be able to explain it to others. You must never lose sight of how important this is to you.

Do not treat it as a lark. Far too much is at stake.

Don't try to make up the rules as you go. You'll make mistakes. There will be too many interested parties, and you'll wind up telling different people different things. If you'll give a discount for cash, decide what it is. How and when will you conduct the bidding? How long do you need to move out?

Put all these things in writing.

Set up your rules and live by them. Never let yourself be bullied into exceptions.

Go for It!

This book is the result of my own success using the 5-Day Plan and the experiences of others who have used it with the same success.

Not one of us was a professional salesperson. We did our homework, followed a series of simple steps and sold our homes in 5 days.

The chapters that follow will lead you through the sale of your home from start to finish. Follow the steps, in order, to the end of the book. Make sure you understand everything all along the way. There will be no time to learn on the job.

In the Appendix are work sheets, sample forms and materials you will need to conduct the sale. Feel free to copy or change them to suit your own style. You will also find a complete checklist; if you don't fully understand an item, reread the section that explains it.

The 5-Day Plan is not difficult. If you follow the steps outlined from this point on, the sale of your home will proceed smoothly.

Remember, you'll be offering the best deal on the market. People will come to you.

WHEN TO BEGIN

WHICH 5 DAYS?

Which 5-day period is best for your sale?

While it's true that more homes are sold in the spring, it's not necessarily true that this is the best time for you. There are more homes on the market in the spring, so there are more ads to compete with. You may want to—or have to—sell at some other time.

If you use the 5-Day Plan, it doesn't matter what time of year you conduct your sale. You can pick almost any Wednesday-through-Sunday period. If you price your home properly, and place your ad in the right places, you can count on 100 telephone calls and 40 inspections at a time that's convenient for you.

I sold my home in the dead of winter. It was raining and snowing during my inspection period. That didn't stop 40 families from coming by.

Holidays are the only exception. Fewer people look for homes during holiday periods. Don't plan your sale for Christmas, New Year's Day or Easter. Don't conduct the sale over any of the three-day weekends—Martin Luther King Day, Presidents Day, Memorial Day, Labor Day. Avoid Thanksgiving week and the Fourth of July week. If you anticipate buyers from specific ethnic groups, check out their holidays and celebrations and plan around them.

The only other thing you should try to avoid is a natural disaster. If you know that a hurricane or flood is heading your way, wait until after it passes to conduct your sale.

Forget about trying to sell your home at a time you think will be good for buyers. When you use the 5-Day Plan, you can sell your home at a time that's good for you.

SELL FIRST?

Let's say you're convinced you can sell your home at almost any time of year. But should you sell before you've bought another home? Or should you buy your new home before you sell the old one?

Everyone will tell you to sell first, then buy.

People will give you this advice because they assume you won't be able to sell your home quickly and you can't afford to own two homes at the same time. They'll also tell you that you can't know what you can afford to pay for a new home before you know what you'll get for your old one.

What your friends and family are really trying to say is, "Don't get squeezed!"

It's true that if you plan to sell your home using the conventional method, and you're not wealthy enough to afford two homes at the same time, you have no practical choice but to sell your old home before you buy a new one. But this is not the most desirable situation. If you sell your old home before you buy a new one, you're just as likely to get squeezed in the other direction. You may have to move out of your current home sooner than you wish, with nowhere to go.

It's much easier to buy a new home if you're not under pressure. You'll buy a better home, in a better neighborhood, at a better price, if you can take your time, walk away from bad deals and carefully think over every step of the process.

If you buy your new home at a better price, you may not need as much money for your old home as you thought. If you buy first, you know exactly how much money you need.

Once again, the conventional wisdom is not always right. If you're not planning to sell your home the conventional way, the conventional wisdom does not necessarily apply to you.

BUY FIRST?

If you buy first and then sell, you can shop carefully, bargain hard and take the time to find a really great deal.

You can make just as much money by buying your new home at a very low price as you can by selling your old home at a very high price. Most people don't seem to realize this. They hold out for an extra thousand dollars on the sale and then, because they haven't left themselves enough time to negotiate, pay an extra five thousand dollars when they buy.

If you can make as much on a good buy as you can on a good sale, should you buy first and then sell? Not so fast. Even if you use the 5-Day Plan and sell your home quickly, things can still go wrong. What do you do if your buyer can't get a mortgage or decides not to buy after all?

If problems arise soon after you conduct the bidding, you can go to the next bidder on the list and simply sell your home for less. Quite probably you can resolve your problem within hours of discovering it.

But if it takes weeks for your sale to unravel, the other buyers can disappear. Then you have to sell your home all over again. Only this time you're behind the eight-ball. Instead of negotiating from strength, you're negotiating from weakness.

Buying first and then selling, while potentially lucrative, is too risky. Selling your old home and buying a new one are so important to your financial future that it's dumb for you to take unnecessary risks.

Don't do it.

THE PERFECT SOLUTION

Using the 5-Day Plan, you can buy and sell at the same time.

Start by setting up the sale of your present home. Have it professionally inspected. Decide what repairs you must make, and then make them. Price your home. Decide where you'll place your ads. Test your sale on your friends and family. Get everything ready.

But don't place the ad.

Go out to look for your new home. Take your time. You're in no rush, so you won't be squeezed in either direction. Go out there and find the right home for you. Negotiate a price. Agree to buy.

Now sell your home.

Everything should be lined up and ready to go. Place your ad in the paper for the next Wednesday through Sunday. Pick up the 5-Day Plan from where you left off. By Sunday you should sell your current home at the best possible price.

While you're selling your current home, your attorney will be working on the contract for your new home. There is no way the contract will be ready for your signature before you've had the chance to conduct your sale.

Tell your attorney to put a clause into the contract that excuses you from your obligation to buy the new home if your buyer fails to purchase your current home by a certain date. The seller won't like this and may want to back out of the deal. But sellers using the conventional method have not seen as many buyers in a year as you'll see in 2 days. Without dozens of offers to select from, the seller will probably end up accepting this contingency. If not, drop the deal.

Your attorney can structure contracts with both the buyer of your home and the seller of the home you plan to buy in a manner that presents no risk to you if a problem develops with either one. Do not put yourself at risk. Maintain a position where you can negotiate from strength with both sellers and buyers.

The ideal situation is to buy and sell at the same time. The 5-Day Plan allows you to do this.

WHAT IF...?

Things don't work out perfectly every time. Some deals fall through.

If the seller of the home you want to buy won't go along with your contingencies, let it go. Don't put yourself in a position where things must go right or you're in trouble. Find another home.

Any seller would prefer to sell without contingencies, but this may not be possible. You may be the first real buyer to come along in more than a year. If you start to walk away, the seller may have a change of heart and find a way to negotiate a contingency. Something is better than nothing.

You should structure the sale of your home so that it will be bought by someone who can close quickly. This will allow you to close quickly on your new home.

But what should you do if, after negotiating a good contract to buy a new home, you discover you can't sell your old home for what you thought you could get? First talk to the seller. Some sellers may be willing to take a little less to get rid of a home that has been on the market too long. If the seller won't budge, give up on the home. If you can't afford it, don't buy it. Go out and find a home you can afford.

And what if something happens to your buyer? What if your sale doesn't go through? It's the same story again. You may be able to negotiate an extension with the seller. Explain what's happened. Sell your home again, and this time seek out buyers who are able to close quickly.

You've negotiated the right to walk away from your new home if the old home doesn't close by a certain day. Exercise your option.

If you've followed my advice and your attorney has structured the deal properly, in no case will you lose more than the cost of your advertising. You may have to change your plans, but you won't lose much money. You can both buy and sell at the best possible time for you. Explain to your attorney what you're doing, and make sure both contracts are written in such a way that you're not at risk.

Do not permit yourself to get locked into a problem that may cost you a bundle.

PRICING IS EVERYTHING

THE RIGHT PRICE

For the 5-Day Plan to work, you must offer your home at the right price. The pricing rule of thumb is simple: *Ask what the buyer wants to pay, not what you want to receive.*

To get the highest price for your home, you must attract a lot of buyers. The only way to attract enough buyers is to advertise your home at a low price. You must honestly evaluate the *absolute least amount* you'll accept and price your home *at this level or less.* When buyers see the phrase "or best reasonable offer," they'll understand you will take even less, if you must, in order to sell your home.

Don't allow yourself to become emotional about advertising a low price. The market will determine the fair price for every home offered for sale.

Your advantage is that, unlike the conventional home-selling process, you'll get more than you ask if your home is worth more than you're asking.

Even if you sell your home "cheap," you'll still put as much or more money in your pocket as you would if you sold your home at a higher price using the conventional method. You'll sell your home quickly, with a minimum of advertising and no broker's commission to pay.

Look at similar homes for sale. Is your price about 10% less? Will every buyer who sees your ad clearly understand that you're offering the same home for substantially less money? Will every buyer understand that this is the best deal out there?

You can't fool the market. If the market says your home is worth less than the lowest price you would possibly consider, then it *is* worth less than the lowest price you would possibly consider. Face it. The sooner, the better.

This may mean you can't afford to sell your home. It may mean you'll have to take less than you want. In either case, don't put yourself through an extended period of torture waiting to get more than your home is worth. It won't happen. Lower the price or get out of the market.

Everything Has a Price

People love to complain that they can't evaluate prices, but most people can and constantly do. "I wouldn't buy that shirt at that price," "That's a great deal" and "I'll take it" are just three expressions of an ability to evaluate price.

What most people really think is that they're capable of evaluating prices established by others but incapable of establishing prices themselves. This is nonsense. The process of establishing a price is almost identical to the process of evaluating a price.

Pricing is not easy. It can even be painful when something with emotional as well as material value is involved. At the very least, it requires a lot of thought.

To price anything:

      1. Pick a price.

      2. Does the price feel right?

      3. If you answer "no," go back to step 1.

      4. Would *you* buy that thing at that price?

      5. If you answer "no," go back to step 1.

Use this technique to establish a price for your home. Begin by considering *possible* prices. If you feel a certain price is right, put it in the back of your mind. Keep thinking about it. Are you *sure* you would buy your home at that price? If the answer keeps coming up "yes," it's time to test your price on others.

Ask your spouse, "Would you buy our home at this price?" Ask your friends, "Does this seem like a great price to you?"

See the Appendix, pages 221–224, for a worksheet to use in calculating your price. Do not place your ad until everyone you ask agrees that you've arrived at an irresistible price for your home.

BALLPARK PRICING

Before you can begin the process of establishing a specific price for your home, you must establish some sort of broad range. This is often called "ballpark pricing."

You know that if you offered your home for $50 you could sell it in 10 minutes. You also know that if you offered your home for $50 million you would never sell it. The right price for your home is somewhere between $50 and $50 million.

Now you have to narrow it down. You already know the value of your home is closer to $50 than to $50 million. But what is it exactly?

Let's say you own the average American home. To begin with, you know it's certainly worth more than $10,000; more than $25,000; more than $50,000; yes, certainly it's worth more than $75,000. You *know* that if you offered to sell your home for $75,000 you'd have to fight off the buyers. On the low end, you *know for sure* your home is worth more than $75,000. But how much more?

Now work on the problem from the high end. A $50 million price is ridiculous. So is $1 million, and $500,000, and $250,000. You know your home won't bring $200,000. Maybe it could have brought $150,000 at the height of the market, but you know you can't get that now.

The truth is, in today's market you'd be happy to get $120,000 for your home, and you'd be thrilled to get $125,000. So your true ballpark range works out to be somewhere between $75,000 and $125,000.

Once you've narrowed the range, there are several different ways to establish the price you will use in your ad. Interestingly, no matter which pricing method you use, they will all lead to the same price.

SLOW DUTCH AUCTION

Most real estate brokers use the ballpark pricing approach to establish a range. But instead of offering the home at a reasonable price, they put it on the market at the top of the range.

If the home doesn't sell in three months, the offering price is lowered. Three months later, the offering price is lowered again. The price keeps dropping until a buyer is found. This is not really pricing. It is the process of conducting a "Slow Dutch Auction."

The Slow Dutch Auction is the reason it takes so long to sell homes the conventional way. Everyone knows it's not smart to buy a home that has just been placed on the market. All you have to do is wait long enough and the price will come down. Many buyers won't even look at a home until it's been on the market long enough for the price to have dropped several times.

A broker would price the average American home in our example at $125,000 and wait to see what it would bring. But similar homes that had been on the market for a longer time would be offered for $120,000, and $115,000, and $110,000.

As the owner of this home, you would come up with all sorts of reasons why it's better than all the others on the market. But buyers would not come to see it. Why should they? No one would consider your home for $125,000 when there was a nearly identical home on the market for $110,000. While you would argue that your home is nicer, buyers would say that it is not $15,000 nicer.

Buyers know your home won't sell at the high price, and they know your home will remain on the market until you drop the price. They know all they have to do is wait and the price of your home will come down to the same level that was actually paid for other homes like yours.

The conventional pricing method, with a high price that slowly drops down to market level over time, is not good for the seller. It puts the seller under inordinate pressure for a protracted period of time. It will invariably net the seller less money than the 5-Day Plan.

Avoid the Slow Dutch Auction.

PRICE POINTS

While sellers establish a ballpark selling range, buyers establish their own ranges. These ranges are determined by "price points." A buyer will decide on a range between $75,000 and $100,000, for example, and then look only at homes listed between those two price points.

Home buyers select price points they feel they can afford. They winnow out homes within these price points until they find the home that offers them the most value at the best price.

Generally speaking, price points for homes occur at 5% intervals. For homes costing around $100,000, price points occur every $5,000. For homes costing around $1,000,000, price points occur every $50,000.

The standard spread between price points is roughly 25% of the total price. Buyers will consider homes that cost from 12½% below what they feel they can afford to 12½% above what they feel they can afford. Buyers who can afford homes costing around $87,500 will look at homes listed in the range of $75,000 to $100,000. Buyers who feel they can afford to pay around $110,000 will look in the range of $100,000 to $125,000.

It's important to understand that buyers know the prices listed in the ads are not the prices they will finally pay. They'll look at homes costing more than they can afford in the hope that the seller may take less. They'll look at homes costing less than they can afford in the hope of getting a bargain.

Since price points occur every $5,000 for homes worth around $100,000, it makes sense for you to choose a price that falls inside the right range.

Pricing your average American home at $126,500 is a bad idea. It falls just above a price point and will exclude many potential buyers. Don't price your home just outside price points. If your pricing calculations work out just above a price point, drop down. Price your home so that it will appeal to the broadest range of potential buyers.

You can't do this if you sell your home the conventional way. If you list your home at a low price with a broker, you're obliged to accept that price if it's offered. That's a disaster for you. Not only must you accept the bargain price, but you must pay a commission on top of it.

This is not a problem if you use the 5-Day Plan. You're not locked into the price you list in your ad. If your home is worth more, you'll get more.

MAGIC NUMBERS

We have all seen magic numbers, and we have all been taken in by them.

"$9.95," for example. "Oh, come on," you'll say. "I hate prices like that. It's really ten dollars. You can't fool *me*."

But these numbers *do* fool us: $9.95 will outsell $10 every day of the week. In our hearts we call $9.95 "nine bucks" and $10 "ten bucks." Don't fight human nature. All homes should be priced at magic numbers.

Pricing at magic numbers shows you're flexible. It's clear to buyers that you've priced your home at a magic number and that the only magic in the number is that it falls inside a price point.

If your price is just above a magic number, buyers will think your home really falls outside their range and you'll be inflexible about dropping it. Don't let them think that.

Within the ballpark range of $75,000 to $125,000, there are many magic numbers, but the most magical is just under $100,000. That's where you'll catch the most buyers. Buyers looking in the $100,000-to-$125,000 range will know they have a bargain here. Buyers in the $75,000-to-$100,000 range will see a home they just might be able to afford if the final price doesn't go outside their range.

By pricing your home just under $100,000, you'll appeal to everyone in the ballpark range you initially identified. If your home is worth more, the bidding will take it above $100,000, maybe to $120,000, maybe even $125,000.

If your home isn't worth $100,000, all the bids will be lower than the price listed in your ad.

When you use the 5-Day Plan, keep in mind that the magic number is only a starting point. It is neither the most nor the least you can get.

If you establish a price using the magic number approach, you want to use the most magical number available. In your case that number is just under $100,000, probably $99,500. This price will allow buyers to bid over the asking price without going over $100,000.

LOWEST COMMON DENOMINATOR

Most people think no other home is exactly like theirs, and from their perspective they're right. In some developments or co-op apartments, the homes are virtually identical; nevertheless, one has a better view, or a tree adds beauty to a particular lawn.

Buyers will factor in everything that is relevant to them and then start shopping for the best home they can afford. After everything else has been considered, price becomes the common denominator, and the lowest price becomes the lowest common denominator.

If your home carries the lowest price of all the homes they're considering, buyers will bid for your home first. On paper, this seems simple and obvious. In practice, people keep hoping that if they offer their homes at a higher price, and wait long enough, someone will finally come around and pay the price.

It doesn't work that way.

If your home is worth around $120,000, similar homes being sold the conventional way will be priced between $110,000 and $130,000, depending on how long they've been on the market. You must price your home under this range so that your home is clearly the best deal on the market.

You might consider $107,500, but this isn't low enough. A buyer who sees a price of $110,000 will offer the conventional seller $105,000 and settle for

$107,500. Your offering price of $107,500 isn't low enough to pull buyers away from the $110,000 home.

How about $105,000? This is still too close to the $110,000 home. Buyers might go to the other seller with a flat bid of $105,000 and point to your ad in the newspaper. The other seller will accept the bid in order to make the sale. Note that this conventional seller, after paying the broker's commission, winds up with just $98,700.

Your lowest common denominator, in this case, is just under $100,000. Buyers selling their homes the conventional way can't compete with this price because they must pay their broker $6,000 of the $100,000 total sale, leaving just $94,000.

Using the lowest common denominator approach, the best price to list in your ad is $99,500—the magic number just below $100,000.

WHAT'S REASONABLE?

No matter how you figure it, the right price for the average American home in our example is just under $100,000, probably $99,500. (Stay away from numbers like $99,999. Too cute.) If your home is worth more, buyers will bid over $100,000. If it's worth less, buyers will let you know that, too.

Don't be greedy. Low prices are much better than high prices. You are well advised to price your home considerably below the lowest amount you think you would accept.

Having used the 5-Day Plan many times, I've developed enough confidence in my ability to price and enough faith in the free market system to allow the market to value whatever I put up for sale. I feel I get more potential buyers this way—and thus a higher selling price. I don't use the word "reasonable" in my ads nor do I post a minimum bid. I say "$99,500 or Best Offer"—and I mean it! I really will take the best offer I get, no matter how high or low it is, and I make that crystal-clear to every caller.

But since this is your first time, and you're understandably nervous, saying that you'll accept only "reasonable" offers should make you more comfortable with the process. Still, you must prepare for the fact that buyers are going to ask what you mean by "reasonable": "Is the amount stated in your ad the minimum you'll take?" "Is $85,000 reasonable?" "Would you take less?" "How much less?" You must be able to answer these questions without waffling.

You use the word "reasonable" to make sure no one can walk off with your $100,000 home for $20,000 or some other clearly unacceptable price. To figure out what's reasonable, start by defining "unacceptable."

An offer of $20,000 is unacceptable, as are offers of $30,000 and $40,000. Your mortgage is $65,000, so your bank won't permit you to sell your home for less unless you make up the difference, and you can't. As a practical matter, any price below $65,000 is unacceptable.

It doesn't take long to know what's unacceptable. It's a little more difficult to figure out what's reasonable. First, add all your expenses to the unpaid portion of your mortgage. After including attorney's fees, advertising costs, transfer fees, repair costs, unpaid taxes, etc., you may decide you won't consider any bid below $75,000. That may be well below what you're hoping for, but it's not unreasonable.

Now turn to your pricing worksheets. When we priced this home, we placed its value in the ballpark range of $75,000 to $125,000. This confirms that while $75,000 is at the low end of the scale, it's not an unreasonable bid. If your minimum acceptable bid is higher than your minimum ballpark price, you'll scare off some buyers. The higher the minimum bid, the fewer buyers will come to inspect your home. Setting the lowest "reasonable" bid far above the minimum you think your home is really worth won't work. It'll probably result in failure to sell your home.

You must tell all potential buyers that you can see the difference between "unreasonable" and "less than I was hoping for." Buyers must understand that you won't accept an "unreasonable" bid, but you're prepared to take "less than I was hoping for." "Reasonable" can't be a floating definition that increases as buyers approach it. Buyers will consider this tactic unethical and stop bidding.

You must define "reasonable" before your sale begins and you must stick to your definition. Always remember the minimum you calculate is not the asking price. Unless you've severely overpriced your home, all bids will be reasonable and you'll get far more than the minimum acceptable bid.

DO YOUR HOMEWORK

INDEPENDENT INSPECTIONS

Before you fix anything, have your home inspected by an independent home inspection company. In some states an independent home inspection is required before a home can be sold, but have one done whether it's required or not. Show the inspection report to all prospective buyers. This will eliminate unexpected—and unpleasant—surprises later.

A qualified home inspection company will provide you with a detailed report, in writing, of everything you need to know about your home. The report will describe the home in all its technical aspects and tell you what things *must* be repaired and what others you might consider repairing.

After the bidding, buyers can confirm that the inspection company is reputable and that it will stand behind the report. Because you'll sell your home so soon after the inspection is completed, the company will have no problem attesting to the accuracy of the report.

Have your home tested for radon. Your buyer (and possibly the buyer's bank) will ask for a radon report, so you should know in advance how it will come out. This is a very simple process, and one you should consider doing yourself. Buy a radon kit at your local hardware store. Follow the instructions carefully, ventilating the test area beforehand in accordance with the instructions. Run the longest test you have time for, then send the canister to the lab for evaluation. You should have the results within two weeks, so allow yourself enough time before your sale. (A sample report is included in the Appendix, page 235.) If your radon count is too high, fix it. Then retest.

If you have a well, have it tested. If you have a septic system, have a percolation test performed. If repairs *must* be made, you can make them before they pop up and kill your sale.

These tests will answer buyers' questions and reduce the time it takes to close the sale. And, because you're paying for tests that buyers normally perform, you make your home even more desirable.

YOUR OWN INSPECTION

After you know what the professionals think about your home, you must honestly evaluate it yourself. Pretend you're a buyer. Apart from the things that *must* be fixed, what things would you *want* fixed?

If your kitchen is so sad that you want to cry every time you enter it, think about some changes. In terms of the initial impression your home makes, the kitchen is the most important room. A good kitchen can sell a mediocre home. You don't have to do a complete makeover. Sometimes simply refacing the counters and cabinets and replacing knobs can turn a disaster into a perfectly acceptable kitchen.

Look at your bathrooms. After kitchens, they're the next rooms checked out by buyers. Remodeling is nice, but resurfacing will do. Fixtures can be replaced at a nominal cost. At the very least, make sure the existing fixtures don't leak.

Do something about the garage and the attic. If you have a garage door opener, make sure it works smoothly. If not, rip it out. You're better off with no door opener than one you must constantly apologize for.

Bring in contractors. Ask them what they think should be fixed. Show them your independent inspection report. Some contractors specialize in preparing homes for sale. They know how to get the best results for the least money.

With contractors' suggestions and the home inspection report in hand, you're in a good position to decide what to fix and what not to fix.

WHAT TO FIX

There are two categories of things you should fix:

    1. Little things that make a big difference.

    2. Big things that make a huge difference.

The rule of thumb here is that everything you fix should raise the selling price by more than it costs. This applies equally to things that *must* be fixed and things that *should* be fixed.

List all the little things around your home that should be fixed. Then fix them all. When people visit, they may see one or two major projects that need redoing, but not dozens of little things.

Some examples of little things that make a big difference: A good paint job will bring more money than it costs. Replace all the old doorknobs and the plates that cover the light switches and electrical outlets. (Do this *after* the paint job.) Tend to leaky faucets, damaged trim, broken doors that don't close properly, broken screens and rain gutters, and clutter wherever it may be found.

Big things to fix are another story. They can be divided into two major categories:

    a. Big things that must be fixed.

    b. Big things that would make your home much nicer if they were fixed.

In the first category, your independent inspection should indicate all the things that *must* be repaired. If your septic system won't pass a percolation test, it must be fixed. If your home is full of radon, it must be fixed. If your electrical system is a safety hazard, it must be fixed.

However, it does not necessarily follow that *you* must fix everything that must be fixed. Failure to fix basic health and safety items will reduce the number of potential buyers and lower the amount you'll get for your home. Fixing some things may cost more than you'll recover in the sale price. Don't kid yourself. Fix the things that must be fixed only if it pays to do so.

In the second category, fix any big thing that would make your home more attractive if you're *sure* it will return two or more dollars for every dollar you spend.

Fixing things is a judgment call you must make to maximize the amount of money you get to keep from the sale of your home. It is not designed to enrich either the contractor or the buyer at your expense. The decisions are difficult because they're hard to quantify, and the people who might be able to help you have a vested interest in the outcome.

What Not to Fix

Why is it that we can live with certain problems for 10 or 20 years and then, when it comes time to sell our homes, think someone else wouldn't live with those problems for a minute?

Don't get involved with rebuilding your entire home, turning it into your dream house, just before you move out. Stay away from major renovations unless you are certain they're necessary. Many buyers have tastes different from yours; they might hate the work you've just done and end up offering less than it cost you. Other buyers would prefer to pay less now and make renovations to their own specifications at a later time when they can better afford it. Still other buyers will be able to do the work themselves for less than it cost you.

Add up the cost of everything you think you should fix before you start. What does the total come to?

You may discover that you plan to do $50,000 worth of repairs on a home you hope will sell for $125,000. I can guarantee that you're better off selling your home for $75,000 as is, rather than spending $50,000, hoping to sell it at the absolute top end of the market for $125,000—and netting the same $75,000.

As noted earlier, if you put your average American home on the market for $75,000, you'll have to fight off buyers with a stick, there will be so many of them. You would show them the inspection report. You would make sure they understood what needed to be done. People would fight for the chance to buy your home. You'd probably sell it for more than $75,000. The buyers would feel that they'd gotten a bargain. You'd net more than you would by fixing it for $50,000 and then trying to sell it for $125,000.

Make major repairs only if you're sure that every dollar you spend will bring back two dollars when you sell.

How to Know

When you sell your home using the 5-Day Plan, you get immediate feedback on how well you've analyzed the problem of repairs and renovations. If you've figured wrong, you may be able to adjust. Buyers can give you their opinions and negotiate directly with you. You have room to maneuver if you've made a mistake.

Let's say you've decided to price your home at $99,500 and you're wondering whether to renovate your kitchen for $10,000. You already know from the section on pricing that $99,500 is the ideal asking price, and you wouldn't want to change that if you could avoid it. You're pretty sure you could get $99,500 with the kitchen as is.

The advertised price of similar homes that have been on the market for nine months and are being sold the conventional way is $110,000. Your home is a great bargain at roughly 10% below this price. If you spend $10,000 on your kitchen, you must sell your home for $10,000 more just to come out even. It doesn't make sense to risk $10,000 just to come out even. You must feel strongly that you'll be able to sell your home for $120,000 to justify renovating your kitchen for $10,000.

Before you spend any money, look at other homes on the market selling for $110,000. Your home, at a selling price of $120,000 with a $10,000 renovated kitchen is no better a deal for buyers than a home costing $110,000, to which the buyer could then add a $10,000 kitchen.

If your home will bring $120,000 with a new kitchen, it will probably bring $110,000 without the new kitchen. You should see a pattern here.

In most cases, major renovation doesn't pay. It's time-consuming, and costly, and will net you no more money.

The rule of thumb here is: *When in doubt, don't do it.*

PUT IT
IN WRITING

Information, Please

Between Wednesday and Sunday, you can expect up to 100 phone calls from potential buyers and as many as 40 families visiting your home during the weekend inspection period.

Any of these people could turn out to be your buyer, so you want to be sure everyone receives the same information.

This means preparing an information packet before the sale begins. At a minimum, the packet should include:

- A quick description and a longer, more detailed description of your home

- Directions to your home

- A disclosure statement

- An independent inspection report

- A radon report

- A copy of your property survey

- The bidding rules

- A mortgage table

Assembling your information ahead of time will allow you and others in your household to field all questions from callers by referring to the information sheets. Potential buyers who come to see your home will have most of the answers to their questions right at their fingertips.

Write down the information exactly the way you want to present it over the phone. Use a separate sheet of paper for each topic and include your address and phone number at the top of each page. Make at least 100 photocopies of each information sheet, using different-colored paper for each. For quick reference, add an index as your cover sheet, with page numbers and page colors beside each topic. The sheets that will be used for supplying information to callers can be stapled together with your phone logs (see pages 133–34). Keep the rest loose so you can set them out in separate piles, one topic to a pile, during the inspection.

Your information sheets will save you a lot of time and trouble. More important, by writing it all down, you can be sure that all prospective bidders are clear about the exact specifications of your home and the rules of sale.

QUICK DESCRIPTION

The Quick Description is designed to give prospective buyers enough information about your home so they can decide if they want to know more.

If you get 100 calls, you don't really want 100 buyers coming to visit your home. You won't be able to spend enough time with any of them. Forty buyers inspecting your home in a single weekend is about the maximum the average-size home can take. The Quick Description will help you cull the 40 potential buyers from the 100 callers.

Write the Quick Description carefully. It should contain the bare minimum every buyer needs to know. Briefly describe the physical features of the house, as well as the property it sits on and its location relative to schools and shopping. Provide the figures for yearly property taxes and how much you paid for the house. See the Appendix, page 227, for additional information to include on this sheet.

After hearing the Quick Description, some callers will know immediately that your home is not for them and will politely tell you so.

Others will want to hear more.

DETAILED DESCRIPTION

Callers who want more detail will happily spend as much time on the phone as it takes to make sure they won't be running around the countryside, like chickens without heads, looking at dozens of unsuitable homes. For these callers, the Detailed Description should furnish as much information about your home as you can muster.

If you don't know the correct real estate terms, the proper name for the construction of your home or some other technical aspect, you'll find this information in the inspection report and in your tax records. Your deed and accompanying surveys should answer the legal questions.

Use the Detailed Description to answer all the specific questions about your house, such as roofing, gutter and siding materials, electrical service, water supply and waste method. Appliances that will be left for the buyer should also be listed. Dimensions for each room in the house should be included, along with features connected with each room such as fireplaces and bathrooms.

For a sample Detailed Description, see the Appendix, pages 229–30.

Bidding Method

The Bidding Method sheet explains exactly how the bidding will work. This is the central feature of your sale. If prospective buyers understand this sheet, they can easily participate in the process.

Be sure to spell out every aspect of the bidding procedure. Tell when bids may be placed and when the round-robin bidding will begin. Explain how the round robin will be conducted.

You should review this sheet with all potential buyers, both over the telephone and when they come to inspect your home.

The Bidding Method sheet I used is included in the Appendix, page 237. If you want to use the same sheet, just use rubber cement to paste your address and telephone number over the example. Then you can photocopy my Bidding Method sheet on colored paper and leave it around your home.

Instead, you may want to use my process as a guide but conduct the bidding in some other way. You may have restrictions that I didn't have, or you may have fewer restrictions than I had.

In any case, make clear how you intend to conduct your sale.

Mortgage Table

Most home owners think if they buy a home for $100,000 they pay $100,000 for the home. If you remind them about their mortgage, they'll say, "Oh, yes, my mortgage is 8%, so my home really cost me $108,000."

But, of course, an 8% mortgage really costs 8% per year on the outstanding balance for a 30-year period. A home owner who buys a $100,000 home with 20% down and a 30-year mortgage will pay a total of $291,323 for that home—before taxes. Add $100,000 in taxes paid over 30 years, and you can see that the $100,000 home actually costs nearly $400,000!

Still, most people will say, after selling that home 30 years later for $250,000, that they made a profit on the deal. (And the government will tax that "profit.")

Many home owners seem to feel that mortgage payments are mysterious numbers only banks can know. You buy a home. You get a mortgage. The bank sends you a coupon book or a monthly bill, and you pay whatever the bank tells you to pay for what seems like the rest of your life.

Getting the right mortgage from the bank is critical. Most people don't realize they can save more by getting a mortgage rate 1/2% lower for 30 years than by negotiating a selling price that's $5,000 lower. They spend all their time haggling with the seller and then accept whatever rate they can get from the bank. The Mortgage Table included in your information sheets (see the Appendix, pages 239–40) will show that getting a mortgage at the lowest possible rate is far more important than paying a few thousand dollars more or less for your home.

For most purchases the difference of a thousand dollars is a lot of money. But on a house, where the thousand dollars is spread out over 30 years and 360 payments, it comes to just $7.50 a month. When buyers understand how little it costs them to jump up one more level in the bidding, they are far more willing to do so.

The more buyers who understand this, the higher the final price is likely to be.

DIRECTIONS

All callers must be instructed in the simplest, most direct way to your home.

Start from a major road that everyone knows. Drive the route yourself before you write down the directions. Is there a new sign you never noticed before? Is the billboard that has been there for 20 years now gone? Is the big white house now a big blue house?

Check out all distances on your car's odometer.

Write out your instructions. (See the Appendix, page 231, for a sample instruction sheet.) Then go out again and follow them yourself. Make sure you haven't missed a step. Make sure the landmarks given are the same ones you notice when you're driving.

Give every caller the same directions.

Don't discuss shortcuts over the phone. Callers who know the area will know the shortcuts. Those who don't know the area are likely to get lost.

When real estate brokers sell homes, they usually take the buyers from home to home. In your case, your directions must get them there.

Full Disclosure

I cannot overemphasize the importance of full disclosure.

You must be sure that every prospective buyer is bidding on the same home. You must point out every problem. You must point out every flaw.

If you fail to disclose everything, the buyers are certain to discover most, if not all, of the problems before the closing. The buyers may then back out of the deal or demand monetary concessions for problems you failed to disclose.

If you disclose everything, the buyers can't demand concessions for shortcomings that were clearly noted in advance. And, if the high bidder starts to behave unethically or unfairly, you can drop to the second bidder, knowing that the new buyer will not find any problems that were previously undisclosed.

Even obvious things should be disclosed. When I was preparing my home for sale, I started to fix the deck, which had some bad planks. The further my contractor went, the more he wanted to repair, and what I thought would be a $100 cosmetic fix was turning into a $2,200 replacement. While the work was being done, a woman called the contractor and asked if my home would be offered for sale. When he said it would, she said she'd be interested in buying it but didn't want the deck rebuilt just as it had been.

I stopped work on the deck and plastered the following sign all over the house.

WHERE'S THE DECK?

My contractor was in the process of rebuilding the deck when the first bid on the home came through with the specific request that the deck not be rebuilt exactly as it had been. So we hauled away the trash and stopped work until we knew who the buyer would be.

The contractor is prepared to finish the job for $2,200. I will have the deck finished and add $2,200 to the bid price if the buyer wishes to have the deck back just the way it was.

Or the buyer can build the deck, or hire someone else to build the deck, or tear down the deck and just put stairs up to the back door.

BID ON THE HOME AS IS—NO DECK!

In the final bidding I could be sure every bidder knew the deck was missing and took that into account.

You will have different problems. Point them out. Don't try to slip anything by. It will only hurt you later.

Failure to disclose everything subjects you to a potential liability for fraud. In fact, an ever increasing number of states *require* home sellers to complete a form that discloses every known defect in their property. The National Association of Realtors is lobbying for disclosure laws throughout the country to protect brokers from the threat of lawsuits if sellers fail to disclose defects.

Many states have voluntary disclosure forms. Many real estate brokers require sellers to complete disclosure forms before they'll list their homes. Whether or not it's required, fill out one of these forms. See the Appendix, pages 233–34, for a sample disclosure statement.

THE AD

THE AD IS KEY

The ad is the most important element of the sale. Without it, there is no sale. Even though it's very small and may look lost in the classified section with many other ads, you must work on it until it attracts every single potential buyer.

Don't try to write the ad while you're on the phone talking to the classified ad department. Figure out everything, including the best features of your home, how you'll abbreviate and all other details, before you call. Type out the ad or use a word processor to see approximately how it will look on the page.

Test the ad on your family and friends. See if they think you've described your home accurately and to its best advantage. They should all say they would call after reading the ad if they were looking for a home like yours.

Besides information about your home, you want to convey the following information:

> 1. You're selling your home yourself. No middle person is helping, so there are no commissions to pay.

> 2. You've priced your home so that it's the best buy on the market.

> 3. If buyers don't agree that you've priced your home at the most attractive level, you're prepared to take even less than the asking price.

4. Your home is open for inspection to anyone who wants to see it between the hours of 10 A.M. and 5 P.M. on Saturday and Sunday.

5. Buyers must hurry if they want your home because it will be sold by Sunday night.

A good ad is critical to finding enough buyers. Spend the time. Do it right.

WHAT IT SHOULD SAY

Follow my formula for writing your ad. Not because I say so, but because it works.

Don't waste your time and money on phrases like "a real charmer" or "too cute to be true." If buyers come to your home and *they* say it's a real charmer, fine, but most people aren't looking for charm or cuteness—they're looking for homes.

Work hard on the part where you describe your home. Mention features you feel will be important to others. Include these essential elements:

1. The location of the home.
2. The fact that you're selling it yourself.
3. A brief description.
   How many bedrooms?
   How many bathrooms?
   Is there a garage?
   Does it have special-purpose rooms? If so, what kind?
      Dining room?
      Family room?
      Entertainment center?
      Utility room?
      Workshop?
      Sun porch?
   Does it have special features?
      Fireplace?
      Swimming pool?
      Tennis court?

4. The amount you hope to get for your home.
5. You'll take the best reasonable offer.
6. You'll sell by Sunday night.
7. The area code and telephone number where someone will
   be taking calls for 5 days.

Write the ad so people understand what your home is really like and will call. Include only the important features that make your home special. There's no need to go into great detail. The purpose of the ad is to get the calls. When you have potential buyers on the phone, you can give them as much detail as they want to hear.

WT YR AD SHD N LL*

The ad below makes every mistake in the book—and some new ones. It looks small on the page. It's unintelligible. It uses the same abbreviation to mean different things. The phone number doesn't have an area code.

N. AtN B/O 5BR 3B HoP Dk P'io DR
D/w/fp LR $99,500 or B/O I-SS 10-5
WBSB Sun THB 869-3138

An ad like this will save the seller around $50 in advertising costs, but it will attract few buyers and cause the home to sell for thousands of dollars less.

Don't try to cram everything you can think of into a tiny ad by using abbreviations no one will understand. Just because brokers' ads are full of code doesn't mean they're good ads. If anyone you test your ad on asks what you mean by an abbreviation, drop it or change it. You're better off with a few understandable words than a lot of gibberish.

Remember, you're writing your ad for people just like you.

---

*What Your Ad Should Not Look Like

WHAT IT SHOULD LOOK LIKE

Basically, your ad should look something like this:

```
NORTH ANYTOWN          BY OWNER
5BR House on Pond    Deck    Patio
Den w/fpl  Din Rm  Liv Rm  3 Baths
   $99,500 or Best Reasonable Offer
      Inspection Sat.–Sun. 10–5
House will be sold by Sunday Night to
Highest Bidder          (608) 555-3138
```

This ad will work in almost any newspaper format. It's clear and concise, and it says everything that needs to be said to get 100 telephone calls.

The formula is simple:

- The location of your home goes in the upper left-hand corner, flush left, in capital letters. The words "BY OWNER," also in caps, go in the upper right-hand corner, flush right.

- The next two lines describe your home. As a rule of thumb, figure that you can get about 35 characters on each line.

- The price and the words "or Best Reasonable Offer" are centered on the fourth line. (Make sure "Best Reasonable Offer" is spelled out. Don't use the abbreviation BRO.)

- "Inspection Sat.–Sun. 10–5" goes on the fifth line, centered.

- "House will be sold by Sunday Night to" goes on the sixth line, centered.

- "Highest Bidder" appears in the lower left-hand corner, flush left. Your telephone number, including area code, is in the lower right-hand corner, flush right.

It's not a tragedy if you add a line to your listing because your home is so feature-laden that two lines of description are not sufficient. But the description of your home is not what will sell it.

The price in your ad is the single most important feature. Be sure it's low enough.

WHERE TO PLACE IT

Your ad will appear for just 5 days, so you can afford to run it in the best places.

What are the best places?

Ask yourself where you'd look first if you were buying a home like yours. Usually, the answer is the homes-for-sale section of the classified ads of one or two newspapers, typically one local and one big-city or regional paper.

The easiest way to judge a classified section is to see how many home-for-sale ads it carries. If it has a lot, join the crowd. If not, keep looking.

Buyers are lazy, just like you and me. They don't want to have to buy three or four newspapers to find homes for sale. They want to be able to pick up a single paper and find all available homes in one place. They soon discover that ads in the smaller classified sections are almost always duplicates of ads found in the larger ones.

By selecting the top local classified section and the big-city or regional classified section, you will appeal to prospective buyers who live near you and to those who live somewhere else. People living elsewhere learn the best regional sources for ads and consult them when they come to look for homes.

It's pointless to advertise in *The Millionaire Times* if your home will sell for $20,000 or to list a multimillion-dollar home in *The Penny Saver*. Advertise where a reasonable buyer for a home like yours is likely to look.

You don't have to place your ad in every publication within 100 miles of your home. Two well-placed ads will draw the same number of calls as 10 ads scattered all over.

When it comes right down to it, there are only a certain number of buyers out there. You want to alert roughly 100 of them to the fact that your home is available and that it's the best deal on the market. Nearly every potential buyer will look first in the publication that offers the most homes for sale.

Homes are being bought and sold everywhere in the country. Each locality has its own method for spreading the word about homes available for sale. Look around until you find the best homes-for-sale advertising in your area. Then use it.

DID YOU DO IT RIGHT?

One of the most attractive features of the 5-Day Plan is that you'll know immediately if you placed your ad in the right place, wrote it well, and priced your home properly. You won't have to sit around for months, wondering.

Your phone should start ringing by 9 o'clock on the first morning the ad runs and continue to ring all day and night for several days after you've sold your home. When you do it right, you know.

If this doesn't happen, you've made some kind of mistake. You have three options:

1. Leave the ad as is and ride out the problem.

2. Cancel the sale and pull the ad.

3. Fix the ad.

You may get away with leaving the ad as is if you're getting slightly fewer calls than you anticipated. You may still find a buyer by Sunday night, but you won't attract as many potential buyers. If you attract a smaller number of buyers, you may have to settle for a lower price.

If you decide you have a major problem that you can't correct, you can yank the ad out of all newspapers and tell anyone who calls that the sale has been canceled. This approach will give you time to analyze the problem. You can carefully decide whether you want to fix the problem and try the sale at another time, sell your home through the conventional approach, or not sell your home at all.

The third option is to determine what the problem is, change the ad, and proceed with the sale.

A VALUABLE EXPERIENCE

Ever since you were little, people have called your failures "valuable experiences." In this case, if you fail to sell your home, you'll gain experience you can put in the bank.

Let's say you advertise your home for $99,500 or best offer, and nobody calls. If this happens, you can be sure the price is wrong. Your home simply isn't worth $99,500, or anything near that figure.

If you'd offered your home at the right price, it wouldn't matter what the ad said. It wouldn't even matter if the phone number was wrong. People would call the newspaper to get the right one. They would find you.

So, if nobody calls, you can be sure you've seriously overestimated the value of your home. You don't have to wait 3 months or 6 months or a year to determine you're asking more than your home will bring. You can learn in 5 days.

This is painful knowledge. You may have to rethink everything. If your home isn't worth what you thought it was worth, you might not be able to afford the new home you were about to buy. Still, it's a valuable experience. Learn from it.

Cut your losses. Don't get yourself in any deeper. Don't bother trying to sell your home at the same price using a different method. A real estate broker will run ads in the same places you ran your ad. If your ad didn't get a response at a certain price, someone else offering the same home at the same price won't get a response, either.

If you're going to have to lower your price later, you might just as well do it now. The 5-Day Plan will earn you the highest possible return on the sale of your home, but it cannot make your home worth more than buyers are willing to pay. Pricing your home at an unrealistically high level will not flush out an unrealistically high bid.

Learn from your experience. Try the 5-Day Plan again. Go back to the pricing section (pages 67–84) and make sure, this time, that you offer your home at an absolutely irresistible price. Then go out there and sell it for the most it can bring!

UH-OH TIME

In the middle of the night before the sale is scheduled to begin, you'll suddenly awake in a cold sweat, sit bolt upright in your bed and begin to murmur, "Oh my God, what have I done?"

Don't worry! This is perfectly normal. It's called anxiety, and it happens to everyone. When it hits, just pick up this book and turn directly to this page to refresh your memory on the following points:

1. *There is _no risk_ to you in this process if you follow my advice and that of your attorney.* Your home may turn out to be worth less than you'd hoped, and you may fail to sell it, but no one can force you to sell your home for a fraction of its true value.

2. *This is _not_ the wildest thing you've ever done.* People have used variations of the 5-Day Plan since day one. It worked then, and it's worked ever since. If you follow the steps in this book, price your home properly and offer it to enough people, you'll sell your home at the highest possible price.

3. *The _worst_ thing that can happen is that you lose a couple of hundred dollars and 5 days of your time.* If nobody calls, you don't sell your home, and you're no worse off than you were before. You may feel a bit foolish, but you know for sure that your home isn't worth what you're asking, and you're in a much better position to make decisions once you know this.

Go back to bed and try to get some sleep. You'll need it so you can better attend to the avalanche of phone calls you will get tomorrow.

THE CALLS

PHONE LOG

If you've offered your home at an irresistibly low price, the telephone will start ringing off the hook first thing Wednesday morning and continue to ring, almost without pause, until long after you have sold your home.

The best way to keep track of the people who call is to record the following in a telephone log:

1. The name and phone number of each caller

2. The name of the family member or friend who spoke to the caller

3. Identifying information and impressions about the caller

Write down as much as possible in the log.

This may seem like a waste of time, but it isn't. You'll be grateful to have callers' names and phone numbers in case you have to let them know about a change in plans. If you have 40 buyers during the inspection, there will be times when two or three families are in your home at once. Things will go more smoothly if you've made notes of their phone calls and can recall a snippet of conversation with them.

Review the log the night before the first day of the inspection. Discuss notes and impressions with other members of your family who may have made entries. You'll find it easier to greet potential buyers at the door if you can put them into context. Someone may say, "Oh, I spoke to your daughter, she was very helpful," and this will be your introduction. If your daughter put information in the log, you might be able to say, "Yes, she mentioned that your son was sick. Is he feeling any better now?"

Keep the telephone log handy during the inspection and refer to it after your initial contact with each buyer. In many cases a quick reference will refresh your memory and give you a handle for the beginning of a conversation.

See the Appendix, pages 241–44, for a sample telephone log.

A FAMILY AFFAIR

A copy of the telephone log should be placed by each phone with a copy of the information packet, so the whole family can participate in this crucial part of the sale.

Make sure everyone realizes that each caller could turn out to be the person who buys your home. Go over all the printed materials together. Try to think of additional questions that callers might ask.

Stress the importance of the phone log. Check each copy during the sale to confirm that family members are filling them out properly.

Review the procedure for speaking to callers. If your children habitually answer the phone with lines like "It's your quarter, start talking" or "Appleby's Bargain Basement," try to dissuade them from this until your sale is over. After the fifth call or so, everyone in the household will become adept at conversing with potential buyers.

The phone will continue to ring on Saturday and Sunday, when you'll be busy with buyers who come to see your home. Set up a schedule beforehand to assign certain times for family members to answer the phone.

When no one will be around to answer the phone, don't turn on the answering machine except in the most extreme circumstances. It's normally better for callers to get no answer, in which case they will almost certainly call back, than to get a machine that might scare them off.

FIRST CONTACT

Give your callers as much time and information as they want. Some will keep you on the phone for half an hour; others will just want the directions and nothing more. The constant repetition may become tedious, but you can't know if the buyer will be the first caller or the hundredth, so you must have a productive conversation with everyone.

How you answer the telephone is the first thing a potential buyer will learn about you. Do nothing to drive buyers away. A nice, neutral "Hello" is a good starting point. The buyer will then say something like "I'm calling about the house for sale." "Would you like the long version or the short version?" is a good reply. It breaks the ice and allows the potential buyer to structure the call.

Regardless of which version they request, start by reading the Quick Description. Make sure you don't sound like an answering machine. Explain that you're reading this part of the script to everyone who calls. After you've finished, pause, and ask if they want to hear any more.

Some will. Some won't.

If they want more information and don't ask specific questions, just continue reading from your script, stopping occasionally to ask if they want to hear more.

After reading from the script, try to engage callers in some personal conversation. By the end of the call, the potential buyer should feel less like a stranger to you, and you should have some idea of who will be coming to visit your home.

Don't forget to ask for the telephone number of every caller who plans to come to your home. You may decide not to give directions *unless* you get the caller's phone number.

Don't allow callers to talk you into an early inspection. If they say they're working on Saturday and Sunday, offer to stay late for them. Early inspections make other people feel that someone has somehow gained an advantage.

Make sure all callers feel they have the same chance to buy your home.

LAST-MINUTE
CONCERNS

FULL HOUSE

Overall, it doesn't seem to matter to buyers whether your home is furnished or empty, although individual buyers may have a preference one way or the other.

If your home is full of valuable antiques, some buyers may overlook flaws in your home because they're concentrating on your beautiful vases or breakfronts. Other buyers, not liking your taste, may be distracted by your furniture and overlook good points in the house itself. They could more easily visualize their own furniture if your home were empty. Most, however, are sophisticated enough to be able to see past the furniture or to be able to envision their furniture in an empty home.

From your perspective, it's simpler to sell an empty home. You don't have to worry about breakage or pilfering. If there is nothing to damage or steal, you can concentrate on the primary job of selling your home.

People relocated by large companies often receive guaranteed minimum prices from their employers for their unsold homes, enabling them to move to new homes before selling the old ones. These people can easily sell their old homes empty.

Most people have no choice. They can't move out of their present home until it's been sold.

If you do have a choice, pick the easy way: empty your home before you sell it. The rest of us are better advised to try to sell our homes as they are.

Either way, it will not change the final price you receive.

Final Touches

Your home must look *great* . . . for 2 days.

When you open your home for inspection, you must not allow prospective buyers to become distracted by little things that might bother them. It's easy to predict what will bother buyers. They're the same things that bother you.

When they first approach your home, everthing should look neat and trim. Your home should look as if you've maintained it well over the years. The lawn should be lush, the flower beds well tended. Shrubbery and trees should be trimmed. The driveway should appear newly surfaced. There should be no bicycles or junk lying around.

The entryway should be inviting, with the outside light in good repair. Address numbers should be clearly marked. The doorknob should shine, the bell should sing.

Upon entering your home, buyers should immediately feel that its owners are people of impeccable taste and breeding (like themselves). Your home should be uncluttered, the windows washed, carpets and floors spotless. Get rid of any extension cords lying around. Neaten shelves and desktops. Clean out the closets. Hang new shower curtains in the bathrooms, put out new towels, and make sure the soap dish doesn't look like something a mad scientist used for his experiments.

Turn on all the lights to make your home bright and cheery. Flowers are a nice touch.

If necessary, cart away extra furniture. Rent a truck for 2 days and put into it everything that detracts from your home. Park the truck at a friend's house during the inspection period.

Organize the attic and air out the basement.

These are all little things. None will cost a lot of money, and all should be done to show off your home to its best advantage. You can do this because you have to make this extraordinary effort for only 2 days.

SECURITY

You're about to allow strangers to come into your home. This isn't something you normally do, and you must prepare for it. This is true whether you're selling your home using the 5-Day Plan or the conventional method.

If you use the 5-Day Plan, you should have around 40 potential buyers and their families trooping through your home during a single weekend. This will involve between 50 and 100 people. You won't be able to stay with everyone all the time; in fact, sometimes they'll want to be off by themselves for private discussions.

Most of these people will be honest, decent individuals. But some will not. By limiting your inspection to 14 hours, spread over 2 days, you limit your risk. You're likely to have many people in your home most of the time, which will further enhance your security.

If you're selling your home before you've moved out, it's prudent to have someone you trust stationed in every room. Your friends should not seem like guards. In a friendly, cooperative way, their presence will discourage mischief.

Open House Signs

Decorate your neighborhood, and any reasonable approach to your home, with Open House signs to reassure buyers who are following your instructions that they're heading in the right direction.

Most buyers will try to see as many homes as possible in a single day. They'll miss some of the homes either because they don't get to them or because they can't find them. Make sure yours isn't one of the homes that's missed. Make it easy to find. When I put up signs, I think of them as clues in a treasure hunt where my home is the treasure and I want everyone to win.

Don't put up your signs until Friday night, or potential buyers will arrive before you're ready for them. Use bright-colored paper for the signs so people looking for them will have no trouble seeing them from a distance. Along with your address, print the words "Open House" and give the time and date of your inspection. Below is an example of an effective sign, with an arrow large and clear enough to be easily followed.

```
+-------------------------------+
|        OPEN HOUSE             |
|           1829                |
|      Long Pond Road           |
|                               |
|      Friday and Saturday      |
|      10 A.M.–5 P.M.           |
|                               |
|           ———————>            |
+-------------------------------+
```

One way or another, these signs will almost certainly generate extra buyers. Some people who haven't seen your ad in the paper will follow the signs to your home. There may be people in the neighborhood who aren't actively looking but who might love to buy your home.

Check your signs throughout the 2 days of your inspection. Replace those that have blown away or been taken down. Double-check to be sure that all signs are pointing the right way. If there is a street that people commonly go down by mistake, put a sign in the street pointing the other way so people will turn around. Guide them back to your home from the point where they made the mistake.

After your sale is complete, take down every sign you put up. Your neighbors will tolerate the signs for 2 days, just as they tolerate brokers' "For Sale" signs, but you have an obligation to retrieve every last one of them by Monday night at the latest.

READY, SET ...

If you've planned, advertised and set up your sale properly, the rest is just a matter of following through on decisions that were carefully made when there was ample time to consider them.

Go over everything in your mind. Run down the checklist at the end of this book. Get a firm grip on which features you want to point out to buyers when they visit.

Make sure your home is ready to accept an onslaught of visitors at the appointed hour. Be prepared for the fact that some will show up earlier than 10:00 A.M. Put out all your paperwork.

Look forward to tomorrow.

Get a good night's sleep.

OPEN HOUSE

SETTING UP

Before people start to arrive, review your phone log. Check names and any notes you made during phone conversations.

Lay out all your printed sheets in separate piles, one topic to a pile. The materials should be placed on a counter or flat surface, face up, so that every buyer can see every sheet. They will take the sheets that are important to them. Almost everyone will take every sheet. They will compare notes with others in their party and will want to discuss some of the materials with you while they are in your home.

Move all pets out of your home before the inspection begins. Some buyers will be allergic to them and will bolt from your home rather than risk the discomfort of exposure. Don't just put your pets in the backyard—yapping dogs and yowling cats will drive some buyers to distraction.

Make everything easy for your buyers. Is the front door hard to get to? Open the door you normally use and steer buyers in that direction. Is it raining out? Park your car(s) somewhere else so that buyers can enter through the garage.

Plan what you'll do if the weather is inclement or some other unexpected event takes place. Let buyers see that these things are not problems in your home. Show them how you've resolved these problems.

A SALE, NOT A PARTY

Don't confuse your home sale with a party. Don't serve tea and crumpets, or anything else. Have your party after you've sold your home. Then you'll feel like celebrating, and you'll have the money to enjoy it.

Don't watch television while your inspection is under way. Do nothing to distract the buyers. "How 'bout those Knicks" is the last thing you want to talk about when you're trying to sell your home.

Set up an "office" in the room where people normally congregate. In many homes, this is the kitchen; in others, it may be the family room or living room. In any event, it should be a central room where you can keep track of who's coming and who's going. This may not be your real office if you have one in your home. Home offices tend to be off the central track, somewhat isolated.

The "office" should have neatly arranged piles of printed sheets. Make sure there are enough seats so that buyers and their families can sit down with you to discuss the questions they undoubtedly will have.

If your home is empty, put a table and some chairs in a central room where you can conduct your business. It should feel comfortable for all involved. You want prospective buyers to sense how good they'll feel in this home if they buy it.

MISCELLANEOUS SIGNS

If you've lived in your home for a certain period of time, you must have noticed that your friends ask you the same questions over and over again: "Where's the powder room?" "Which door leads to the playroom?" "How do you get to the basement?"

You know what the questions are concerning your home. During the inspection, however, you won't get the opportunity to answer every question for each potential buyer. Anticipate the questions and put up signs before buyers enter your home.

When the sale begins, you may find that you didn't cover all the questions, Some things that are clear when you live in a home are not at all clear to someone who is quickly inspecting the home. If several buyers ask the same question, put up another sign to avoid the confusion.

For example, in my home, the shower in the downstairs bathroom was right behind the entry door. When you opened the entry door, you covered the shower. If you closed the entry door while you were inside the bathroom, you exposed the shower and there was no problem. But buyers going through my home typically just stuck their heads into the bathroom, never entering far enough to close the door and never seeing the shower. They thought it was just a half-bathroom and suspected me of misrepresenting my home.

As soon as I recognized the problem, I made the following sign and put it on the bathroom door.

Subsequently, several buyers commented on the sign. They told me they never would have seen the shower if I hadn't put up the sign. More important, the fact that the downstairs bathroom had a shower was a significant factor in their consideration of my home.

The sign was posted in the middle of the outside of the bathroom door at eye level. No adult could miss it. (Kids didn't need it. They peeked everywhere and hid in places that adults couldn't find. Every kid found the shower without the benefit of a sign.)

WELCOME

If possible, personally greet all prospective buyers who come to inspect your home. Make all who enter feel welcome. Never allow buyers to feel they're intruding on your space or distracting you from something else you'd rather be doing.

Don't worry about too many buyers showing up at the same time. It doesn't hurt if they see that there are plenty of other real people interested in your home.

Ask the first arrivals if they had any trouble with your instructions. This is another easy way to start a conversation, and their observations can be very helpful. If someone got lost, find out where so you can give better instructions to future callers or put up more signs.

After chatting for a minute, it's time to turn to their reason for coming— the fact that you'll sell this home by the end of this weekend. Show them your home. Answer every question. Point out your information sheets.

If the sheets are color-coded, you can know from across the room which sheets are being read. If you see buyers lingering on specific sheets, you can approach them and ask if they need any help with those topics. This is another device that will enable you to start a conversation with a potential buyer.

Always remember that your primary goal is to sell your home. You did not invite these strangers to discuss sports or politics. Stay focused. Within a few hours, you'll develop your own style of greeting people and speaking with them. You'll know what works for you and what doesn't. You'll develop the ability to hit all the highlights in your printed materials.

You'll be sure your home was displayed in its best possible light to enough real buyers to fetch the highest possible price in the current market.

RATING THE BUYERS

Taking Stock

In a conventional real estate sale, you rarely have a multitude of buyers at any one time. Your broker presents a buyer. The buyer offers a deal. You decide whether to accept or reject the deal that is offered.

The buyer may propose a crazy deal that concludes with your receiving two toads and a chicken as a down payment. That may be the best deal you can get, and you may decide to take it. If you reject the deal, there's no telling how long you'll have to wait for the next deal to come along.

But when you sell your home using the 5-Day Plan, you'll be offered many different deals at the same time. You can pick and choose what is best for you. Some may offer more money in return for partial owner financing. Some may offer cash in return for a lower price. Most will opt for conventional bank mortgage financing.

You must know what you want. You must think about it and figure it out in advance. During the final 5 days, you won't have the time to calculate.

From the 40 buyers who inspect your home, you can expect a dozen bids, six of which should exceed the asking price.

If you have a preference for one type of buyer over others, or you're prepared to make financial concessions to get a faster closing, let this be known to all buyers before the bidding begins. Some may have the ability to fit into your preferred category if they know this will make it easier for them to buy your home.

QUALIFIED BUYERS

In conventional real estate sales, it's necessary to "qualify" buyers quickly. Stripped to its essentials, this means that there is no point in showing a home to buyers who lack the means to pay for it.

Real estate brokers talk about "qualified buyers" as though they have some magical power to divine who is willing and able to pay. In most cases, this is based on a little questionnaire, filled out in the broker's office, that's used to calculate the maximum amount the buyers can borrow from a bank if all the answers on the form are truthful.

When you conduct a 5-Day sale, you have neither the time nor the inclination to qualify buyers. All are welcome. The more buyers you have in your home, the better. You need only qualify the successful bidder, not each initial caller.

Some buyers will tell you their bank has "prequalified" them for a mortgage loan up to a certain amount. This is of limited value to you. If the bank doesn't feel your home is worth the amount you and the buyer have agreed upon, it will not provide the mortgage money. End of conversation.

No buyers are qualified until you have their money, and don't let anyone tell you otherwise. People who can afford your home may change their minds at the last minute. People who can't afford your home may find a way to buy it if they want it badly enough.

As far as you're concerned, the speed with which you conduct the sale separates the qualified buyers from the unqualified buyers. If the top bidder is unable to come up with the money, you immediately drop down to the next bidder. The only truly qualified buyer is one whose money is already in your hands. Everyone else is a maybe.

Don't be prejudiced against any potential buyer. The more bidders you get, the better you'll do.

Some people who don't appear to have two nickels to rub together turn out to be worth enough to buy both you and your home. Other people, who you are sure are "perfect," turn out to be just "tire kickers" with nothing better to do on a weekend than look at homes they could never afford.

Don't guess who is who. Treat everyone who takes the trouble to answer your ad with respect. Once under way, the process moves along so quickly that the qualified buyers separate themselves from the tire kickers without any help from you.

CASH BUYERS

What is cash worth?

If your buyer pays cash, you don't need the approval of a third party to conclude your sale. There is no bank or mortgage commitment involved; in other words, there are fewer contingencies to worry about.

Cash deals go fast. The buyer who claims the ability to pay in cash can be qualified very quickly. No one but the buyer will evaluate whether your home is worth the bid price. You can move right to the closing.

In the bidding process, you may want to give preference to people who can pay cash. There are surprisingly many of them. Some may have parents who can put up cash while they apply for a mortgage. Others may have just sold their home. Then there are those with cash businesses who may have difficulty obtaining a mortgage but who have plenty of cash on hand.

Before I sold my home, I calculated that it cost me $100 a day to hold on to it. Mortgage approval at that time was averaging 60 days. So I told all buyers that I would give a $6,000 discount for cash. I sold my home to a cash buyer, and we closed less than three weeks after the sale. Less than a month after I started the process, I had cash in hand.

The second bidder placed a bid $5,500 higher than the cash bid I accepted but needed time to get a mortgage. I took the cash. If it took 60 days to get a mortgage and then an additional three weeks to close, I would have kept

$500 less. If the second bidder had been unable to get a mortgage, I would have had to sell my home all over again.

If you prefer cash buyers, let all bidders know so they'll understand how this will affect the bidding process.

E BUYERS

...e with cash. They must go to a bank
...who have a longstanding relationship
...ge approval in 15 minutes. But you will
... this.

...o to the bank, fill out forms and then wait.
...their financial references to establish their
...the bank will want to look at the home to
...an the amount of the loan. These procedures
..., depending on how great a backlog the bank
has at the time.

In most cases, if the buyer is unable to get a mortgage within a given period, the sale may be voided and you may have to sell your home all over again.

"Prequalified" mortgage buyers are buyers who have already started the mortgage process. They went to the bank before they started looking for a home. They have already filled out the financial forms and the bank has already checked them out. The bank has agreed to lend them money up to a certain limit.

Your home is the collateral for this mortgage loan. The bank will want to take a look at it to make sure it's worth what the buyer will pay. Neither you nor the buyer has any control over this process. Sometimes the bank will not give a prequalified buyer enough money to buy your home. Anticipate that it will take 30 to 60 days for most people to get a mortgage, even if the bank knows the buyer and has already authorized the loan.

If the bank refuses to give your buyer a large enough mortgage, your buyer may be unable to buy your home. In that case, it may be necessary to offer your home to the next buyer on the list.

SOPHISTICATED BUYERS

Most buyers are relatively inexperienced. They have neither bought nor sold a great number of homes.

This doesn't mean, however, that you won't encounter a group of sophisticated buyers when you conduct your sale. Some will be real estate brokers; others will be out-of-work contractors; still others will be old-fashioned speculators. These people are professionals who earn their living by spotting underpriced real estate and buying it. A certain number of them will show up on your doorstep because there is the potential to buy your home at a discount.

Don't think of these buyers as hungry sharks waiting to feed on you. They are good for you in many different ways. They don't inspect overpriced homes because they can't make money on those homes. By their presence they validate your asking price.

The professionals will point out everything that's wrong with your home. Of course, everything they mention should already be taken into account in your disclosure statement. Inexperienced buyers who overhear your conversations with the professionals will be reassured that you've disclosed everything and they don't have to be experts to know your home is a good deal.

Sophisticated buyers will not be shy about leaving bids. They understand better than unsophisticated buyers the value of your home. They will leave bids that are good for you and great for them.

If there are many buyers for your home, the sophisticated buyers will push up the price until it approaches the retail level and then leave the unsophisticated buyers to fight it out.

If retail buyers drop out of the bidding, sophisticated buyers will remain. They'll be there to buy your home if they can buy it at their price.

PROTECTING THE BROKER

Real estate brokers who see your ad will know you're offering your home at a great price. They'll want to bring their clients around to see it. And they'll want you to pay them a commission if their client buys your home.

This is called "protecting the broker."

Don't do it!

You cannot protect the broker. You've priced your home on the basis of no broker. You can't sell your home at a discount and then pay a commission.

Instead, tell the broker to bid on behalf of the client with the understanding that the buyer, not the seller, will pay the broker's fee in the event of a sale.

Treat the broker's client like any other buyer.

WHAT AM I BID?

HELP THE BUYERS

Few people think about the mechanics of buying a home, except during that brief time when they're engaged in the process. Even then, they allow themselves to be herded like sheep, from one home to the next, by real estate brokers who may not be much more sophisticated than they are themselves.

Many buyers will ask you to help them bid. If they trust you, they'll correctly perceive that they're bidding not against you but against the other people they see admiring your home. They know that *somebody* will buy your home by Sunday night.

Be straight with your buyers. Give them some sense of what you think your home will actually go for so they can determine if they're in or out of the bidding. If you have a minimum bid, let them know. If you don't have a minimum, let them know that, too.

If any buyers really want your home but don't know what to bid, ask them to leave a bid that you can be sure won't be the high bid. Tell them you'll call when the inspection is over to advise them of the high bid and to allow them to enter the bidding if they wish to do so.

In all likelihood you'll wind up with a group of buyers clustered around some buying price. At today's interest rates, bidding another thousand dollars will cost a buyer only $7.50 a month. Most buyers would agree it's dumb to lose the home they want for chump change.

The section called "For Buyers Only" (pages 207–15) will help buyers understand the bidding strategy. Show them this section or photocopy the pages and make them part of your written materials.

The 5-Day Plan works because it's simple and fair. It results in the best deal for both buyer and seller. If prospective buyers understand this, they will be more willing to participate in the process.

HONESTY *IS* THE BEST POLICY

Buyers will not bid unless they feel they can trust you. You must conduct your sale with your cards face up at all times. You must be totally honest.

During the inspection you are trying to establish an order for the round-robin bidding that will take place Sunday evening. Do not open your home for additional inspection after the inspection period has ended for all other buyers. Do not allow buyers who have not seen your home to bid on it.

Tell each prospective buyer that after the inspection period is over you will call everyone who bids in order from the highest to the lowest bid.

The bid can be a penny, but this will put the bidder at the bottom of the list. If someone wants a call but doesn't want to leave a bid, just write down a penny next to the name.

When the round-robin bidding begins, call each buyer in turn. Anyone who does not wish to raise the bid is dropped from the process with the understanding that if higher bidders fail to close on your home, it will be offered to the next bidder on the list, and so on, for a certain number of top bidders.

Some people will ask how they can know that the bidding is being fairly conducted. The best answer is that it's in your best interest to conduct the bidding fairly.

If you can create a pool of legitimate buyers, all within a few thousand dollars of each other, you'll probably be able to sell your home to one of them.

If you stretch out the top bid by creating false bids, you run the risk of inadvertently outbidding your top bidder and not selling your home at all. The principal factor that works in your favor is the speed with which you're able to locate multiple buyers for your home, and your ability to get many bids close together.

Having multiple buyers available is your protection against winding up over a barrel when dealing with one bidder separated from the pack by false bidding. False bidding will backfire more times than not.

Decide what you're willing to accept for your home. Make it clear to bidders where the floor is. Conduct the sale honestly. Take what you can get.

NOT AN AUCTION

*P*lease *understand that you are not running an auction.* Auctions are professional sales; they are not for you and me. They're conducted according to strict laws promulgated by the state and firm rules established by sellers.

Licensed professionals conduct auctions. You and I have neither the license nor the skill to be an auctioneer.

During an auction, so many things are sold over such a short time that amateur buyers don't know what they're doing. They're intimidated by the rules and don't know the laws. They can't keep up with what's going on. As a result, most ordinary people hire professionals for both selling and buying at auction.

Auctions are characterized by inadequate inspection times, strict rules, no time to think during the process, and cash on the barrelhead. Ordinary people rarely buy or sell anything of value at auctions without the help of professionals.

Professional real estate developers who get into trouble will sometimes resort to auctions to unload as many properties as quickly as they can. These developers *always* employ professional auctioneers, who receive sizable fees. Many properties are offered in a single day, one right after the next. Most properties have unstated minimum prices below which they will not be sold.

This is not what you are doing. You are offering your home in a free market. You take bids at a leisurely pace. Potential buyers have enough time to carefully consider what they are doing. You have enough time to consider the bids. You talk to each bidder individually and make sure each understands exactly what is going on. You come to an agreement as a result of the free market process, but neither party is legally obligated.

Do not call this process an auction. It will scare off many potential buyers. They will see you as a professional and themselves as amateurs. If they think you have the upper hand in the process, it will adversely affect your sale.

OPEN VS. SEALED BIDDING

In open bidding, all bids are disclosed to all buyers so that someone who really wants your home can raise the bid. In sealed bidding, each prospective buyer submits one bid sealed in an envelope; all the envelopes are opened at a certain time, and the highest bidder gets the home.

Stay away from sealed bidding. It's not fair to either the buyer or the seller.

Sealed bidding will be proposed by buyers who hope to "steal" your home for a ridiculously low price because no one in a sealed bidding situation knows what to bid. People who really want your home do not favor sealed bids because they have to offer much more than they might otherwise bid to guarantee that their bid will be the highest.

Your job is to sell your home for the highest possible price and to attract the largest number of potential buyers so that if one falls through you can simply go to the next one on the list.

In sealed bidding, the high bidder may be $10,000 or $20,000 higher than the next bidder. In this situation, you'll bend over backwards to close the sale with the high bidder, possibly extending the time for so long that you lose the possibility of selling to any other bidder. Then what do you do if the top bidder drops out? For all you know, the second or third or fourth buyer was working in collusion with the top bidder. Remember, you don't really know any of these people, and situations will develop if you allow them to.

On the other hand, if the bidding is open, all bidders know they're in the right ballpark. The top bidder knows there's another bidder within $500 and a half-dozen bidders within $3,000. This discourages collusion and allows the top bidder to know that the high bid was not out of line. All bidders will know that many other people looked at your home and agreed it was worth roughly the same price.

CRAZY BIDS

During the inspection, somebody will poke you in the ribs and say, "Yeah, but what if I offered you a million dollars for this home, right on the spot. I'll bet you'd take it!"

Wrong.

If someone offers you much more than you know your home is worth, something is wrong with the deal. The check will be bad; the money counterfeit; the buyers will try to change the terms; the bank won't grant a mortgage. It will almost certainly fall through. You'll be left high and dry—and it will serve you right!

You wrote the rules for this sale. You play by your rules. There is no reason for anyone to offer you a million dollars on the spot for a home that's worth only $125,000. If it happens, it's a trick.

In all probability, no one will offer you a million dollars for a $125,000 home, but someone could say, "I'll give you more than anyone has bid so far if you stop the bidding and let me have the home right now."

Don't do it.

Instead of six buyers, you will have just one. If something happens to that buyer, you will have none. People who came to see your home only to be told that it was already sold are not likely to come back a second time. Keep in mind that the buyer pool has only a certain number of buyers in it and that you may have to jump into the pool a second time.

You have an obligation to all the people who called to follow the rules you outlined to them over the phone. This will work best for them. It will work best for you.

THE ROUND ROBIN

The round-robin bidding is a critical period in the sale. It goes very fast. It is very important.

Give yourself some time between the end of the inspection and the beginning of the round robin. The last potential buyer may leave late. You may want to have a quiet dinner with your family. You'll want to unwind before you set up your bidding sheets (see the Appendix, pages 250–55) and consult your telephone log for notes on each bidder.

Transfer all notes to the bidding sheets. You will work only from those sheets once the bidding gets under way.

Call the high bidder exactly when you said you would. Review with the high bidder how many other bidders are in the process, how many you regard as serious bidders, and how you think the bidding will go.

Help the high bidder to use the first-bid advantage. If the high bidder is only $250 or $500 above the next bidder, it's fairly certain that the second bidder will make a higher bid. The high bidder may want to advance the bidding to preempt other bidders.

When the first bidder has settled on a bid, call the second bidder. Tell the second bidder how many other bidders are in the process, how many you regard as serious, and how you think the bidding will go.

Continue this process until you've contacted all the bidders. Some will drop out immediately. Others will want to work with you on the phone. On average you'll spend five minutes with each bidder. Tell each approximately when you expect to be able to call back.

When buyers drop out of the bidding, tell them you'll call them back after the bidding is concluded to advise them of the final status. Do not allow a bidder to come back into the bidding after dropping out.

Don't rush any bidder. You are discussing a major purchase. The actual bidding can create unexpected situations, so give each buyer enough time.

Once every bidder has been given a chance to bid, call the first bidder again. If no one has made a higher bid, the first bidder can buy your home at the bid price. If there has been a higher intervening bid, give every bidder the opportunity to top that bid.

Continue this process until a high bid emerges, and no other bidder wishes to top it.

Then call all the bidders to tell them where their bid falls in the final bidding order. Tell each that if the high bidder fails to close on your home you will immediately call the second bidder, and then the third. Tell bidders they'll have the opportunity to buy your home at their bid price if bidders at higher prices are unable to close in accordance with the rules on the Bidding Method sheet.

THE LEGAL END

WHY YOU NEED AN ATTORNEY

When you've concluded the bidding, you have nothing more than a good-faith agreement with the buyer. If either you or the buyer backs out of the deal, there may be hard feelings but there will be no legal ramifications if you have obtained proper legal advice from your attorney.

Up to this point I've advised you to do everything yourself. You price your home, set up the ad, decide what should be fixed, answer the telephone, run the inspection and conduct the bidding. You can do all this yourself because you have nothing to lose. Your common sense and self-interest enable you to make decisions and take action as well as anyone else. If you change your mind, you can stop the process at any time.

But don't think just because you've successfully avoided the expense of a broker, you can also avoid the expense of an attorney. This is a false economy. Too much is at stake. Because each state has its own laws governing real estate sales and auctions, an attorney should be consulted at the outset to advise you about the particular ramifications of following this plan in your state.

After the sale of a home has been negotiated, a very precisely choreographed dance begins between seller and buyer. This is when the buyer reconsiders, asks for concessions, tries to include things that were never part of the deal. This happens whether the home has been sold the conventional way or using the 5-Day Plan.

For a while, though, your position is stronger if you've sold your home using the 5-Day Plan. Both you and the buyer know that other bidders are eager to buy your home if the deal falls through. In a conventional sale, you and the buyer may know this is the only serious offer you've received.

Your negotiating position deteriorates as time passes and underbidders find other homes to buy. Make the time between the bidding and the closing as short as possible. Be sure everything is done in a legal and binding manner.

This is where your attorney comes in. From the moment you arrive at an agreement, both you and the buyer should use only professional intermediaries. Your attorney will qualify the buyer, protect your interests, certify that everything has been done legally, and speed up the process in ways that would be difficult for you if you were handling things yourself.

WHAT ATTORNEYS DO

Different attorneys specialize in different things. You don't need a brilliant trial lawyer to close a home sale. You need someone who is familiar with real estate law and who knows how to set up closings. Your attorney must be able to coordinate quickly all the events that will occur before you can consummate your deal.

If you don't already have an attorney, ask friends and relatives for recommendations. Ask them if their attorney handled their sale in a professional manner. Were there any snags that could be attributed to their attorney? Was everything done quickly and explained fully? It's a good idea to interview every recommended individual until you find someone you're comfortable with.

You and your attorney should establish timetables. If your attorney fails to contact the buyer's attorney or to produce contracts for the sale of your home and otherwise perform in a timely and professional manner, find another. Right away.

Immediately after you've negotiated your deal with the buyer, get the name and phone number of the buyer's attorney and give these to your attorney along with all details about the conditions of the sale.

The two attorneys will then work out everything between themselves. They will contact the banks, arrange for title searches and title insurance, write up all contracts, calculate conveyance fees due to state and local governments, and come up with a simple piece of paper that explains how much you'll get out of the deal when all is said and done.

You can rate the attorneys by how quickly and smoothly everything moves. If the process starts to bog down, and you know it's not your attorney's fault, the problem has to be with the buyer or the buyer's attorney. Seriously consider contacting the next bidder on your list if this happens.

Sometimes, at the closing, all sorts of things pop out of the buyer's attorney's attaché case. Things you never saw before. Things your attorney never saw before. The buyer may feel you'll sign anything that comes along to protect the sale of your home. Don't fall into this trap. Listen to your attorney. Don't sign any pieces of paper your attorney advises you not to sign.

Attorney fees vary in different parts of the country. They should run between $250 and $750, depending mainly on where you live. If your closing is very complicated, your fees may run higher. Try to keep the closing as simple as possible by culling out complicated deals at the time of the bidding. Make sure the attorneys and the bank agree to everything in advance, before the closing.

GOING TO CONTRACT

The contract sets up the closing. You use the contract to ensure that the closing will come as soon as possible after the sale. It's in your interest, both financially and psychologically, to close on your home quickly.

Among other things, the contract will stipulate:

- The amount of the sale

- The timing of the sale

- The timing of transfer of funds

- What is included in the sale

- What is excluded from the sale

- How the title will be conveyed

- How taxes, assessments, delivered fuel and miscellaneous fees on the property shall be apportioned

- Who is responsible for insurance

- The condition of the premises

- The location and timing of the closing

- Obligations in case of a default

- Everything else that may in any way affect the sale

In most cases, your attorney will write the contract and send it to the attorney for the buyer. The buyer's attorney reviews the contract with the buyer to verify that everything in it agrees with the buyer's understanding of the deal. They may ask for changes or modifications.

When you and the buyer and both attorneys agree to the contract, you and the buyer sign it. Its provisions then go into effect, and the remainder of the sale is conducted in accordance with what's in the contract.

Sometimes the contract requires a down payment to be made immediately. This down payment may range from $1,000 to around 10% of the purchase price and is kept in escrow by your attorney. The down payment (often called "earnest money") is one way for you to determine quickly whether or not the buyer intends to go through with the sale.

Usually the down payment is not refundable if the buyer fails to live up to obligations set forth in the contract. These obligations are to seek a mortgage within a certain amount of time, to inspect the property on a timely basis, and to be prepared to close on the house by a certain date. If the buyer is unable to get a mortgage, or discovers that you've materially misrepresented your home in any way, the deal is off and the down payment is refunded.

Your attorney's job is to write the contract and get the down payment as quickly as possible. An experienced attorney will have been through this process a hundred times and should know if the requests made by the buyer are customary.

"Putting it on paper" is a very important safety check for both you and the buyer. It forces the buyer to come up with some of the money. It lets you know immediately whether the buyer is serious or not. It establishes a timetable for the sale. And it confirms that everyone understands and agrees to the deal.

THE CLOSING

Real estate brokers talk about the closing as if everyone knows what it is, when in fact most people have no idea.

Basically the closing is the final meeting between you, your attorney, and the buyer and buyer's attorney, at which you get the money and the buyer gets the home. Dozens of pieces of paper are signed (all of which your attorney will explain to you during the meeting prior to your signing).

Other people may be there, representing title insurance companies, banks, and any other parties that have an interest in what is going on. If both you and your spouse are selling the home, you both should be there. The same is true for the buyer if more than one individual is involved.

Cash closings are generally quicker and less complicated than closings where a bank is involved. In a cash closing, there is no bank mortgage.

The closing may be held in an attorney's office, in a room made available by a bank, in a title insurance company room, or anywhere else that has a large table with enough chairs, a degree of privacy and a nearby photocopy machine.

The closing should be smooth and painless if the attorneys have done their jobs properly. There should be no surprises.

The buyer's attorney or bank should give your attorney a certified check. Your attorney will write a check to your bank to pay off your mortgage; your attorney will write checks to cover all city and state taxes; your attorney will receive a check from you to cover closing fees, or will deduct the fee from the check you finally receive after everyone else has been paid.

Within an hour, or an hour and a half, you should have in your hand one of the biggest checks you've ever seen and the buyer should own your home.

It doesn't always go this way. It ain't over until you have that check in your hand! Sometimes homes fail to close for the weirdest reasons. Sometimes the buyer simply doesn't have the money (and never told you or anyone else). Sometimes there is a snag in the title search or title insurance. Sometimes someone gets cold feet and the whole deal falls through. Sometimes these things happen inside that little room, with all those people, at the very last possible moment.

You can fail to close even when the most diligent attorneys are involved. Try to structure the closing in such a way that if it falls through, for any reason, you're not financially ruined.

FUNDAMENTAL
PROBLEMS

FIX IT

Because the 5-Day Plan yields results so quickly, it's possible to fix problems before they ruin your sale. If you don't receive any calls by noon on Wednesday, there is a problem, assuming you have advertised in periodicals that reach potential buyers on Wednesday morning.

Fortunately, there is still time to change the ad by either Thursday or Friday, and that's soon enough to find most available buyers.

The 5-Day Plan will work every time if you use it properly. It requires only that you make your home the best deal on the market at the time it's offered. If you set up your ad correctly, people will beat a path to your door. Figure out why the ad isn't working.

First, buy copies of the periodicals in which your ad appears. Make sure your ad is in the right place and that it says what you want it to say. Check that the telephone number is printed correctly (and that your phone is working properly). Either of these is easy to fix. However, your mistake may be elsewhere.

If you placed the ad in the wrong periodical, shame on you. You didn't do your homework, and you have no one to blame but yourself. Figure out what the right place is, and run your ad there.

If you didn't write the ad properly, fix it. Test your ad on family and friends all over again to be sure it appeals to buyers and is easily understood.

In 99% of all cases, however, the problem with the ad is that you didn't price your home properly. You listed the price you hoped to receive instead of the price buyers hoped to pay. You did not made it clear to potential buyers that your home is absolutely the best deal on the market.

Change the price in your ad. Pretend it was a misprint or that someone else made a mistake. Your price must look good to every potential buyer. If the price is right, the buyers will call.

DO IT OVER

Some situations can't be fixed. Both man-made and natural disasters fall into this category. In these cases it is wise to reschedule your sale for another 5-day period.

No one will blame you for rescheduling your sale in the face of an earthquake or tidal wave. Everyone will understand if you change the sale date because there's a major riot, or the country goes to war, or the stock market crashes. These are times when people aren't thinking about buying homes.

Sometimes it's the weather that just doesn't cooperate. We're not talking about a little spell of bad weather here. Normal seasonal weather shouldn't make much difference. It poured on the first day of my inspection and snowed on the second. People came the first day to see if my home leaked in the rain. (After that, they could be very sure it didn't.) On the second day, snow made my home look great. I don't think anyone stayed away because of the weather. Maybe they all thought others would stay away and they could buy the home for less.

But if there's an unexpected hurricane or blizzard on the weekend you're selling your home, that's a different story. You must change your plans.

If you must schedule a "do over," first look at the calendar. The best time to reschedule the sale would be the following weekend. But if the problem will last more than a week, or a holiday is coming up, or the next weekend is inconvenient, you may have to postpone the sale for more than a week.

Tell anyone who calls why you've rescheduled and when the sale will be held. Then go through your regular drill, reading from your information sheets, entering the calls in your telephone log, and getting the callers' phone numbers in case there's another change of plans.

If you kept a good phone log, you can call all interested parties to advise them of the new date for the inspection and sale. If people come whom you couldn't reach, make them feel welcome to inspect your home and explain why you've postponed the sale. Tell them you called everyone who left a phone number and you're sorry you were unable to reach them.

Start all over the Wednesday prior to the new sale date. You'll have to place your ad again. This is unfortunate, but it's much less costly than trying to sell your home in the face of a disaster.

From this point on, run your sale as if nothing had happened.

FORGET IT

What if you offer your home for sale, attract a sufficient number of bidders, and none of them offers enough money to pay off your current mortgage? This is a fundamental problem that requires serious thinking.

Please note, we're not talking about your home failing to attract bids near your asking price. We're talking about a home that's worth less money than you owe the bank.

Under these circumstances, if you sell your home for the most you can get, not only will you lose your entire down payment, and all your equity, but you'll actually have to pay the bank more money than you'll receive from the buyer!

Given this situation, it doesn't pay for you to sell your home now, regardless of what sales method you choose.

Sometimes the best thing is to just continue living in your present home and wait for times to improve. All you have to do is make your mortgage payments. You don't have to incur the expense of moving. You don't have to put up any additional money. You can just continue living the way you've been living in the home you've been living in.

With interest rates down, you might want to refinance your home at a lower rate. But you won't be able to get as large a mortgage as you presently have, so you'd have to put up cash to exercise this option. You may choose to do this, but be aware that it's the same as selling your home and paying the bank the difference.

If renting or buying another home makes more sense than keeping your present one, it's time to start negotiating with the bank that holds your mortgage. If you've put your home on the market using the 5-Day Plan, you have a good idea what it will bring. Together, you and the bank may be able to structure a deal that works for both of you.

FOR BUYERS ONLY

A Word to Buyers

There is nothing in this book that sellers must keep from buyers. In fact, some sellers may leave the book lying around so that buyers who are not familiar with the 5-Day Plan can better understand how it works.

Buyers must understand they are not competing with the seller for the home. They are really competing with other buyers for the privilege of buying it. The seller has decided to sell a home for what it will bring. The seller has attracted enough potential buyers so that the free market will work. Each buyer must develop a bidding strategy.

There is nothing legal or binding about this bidding process. A potential buyer can bid anything and then say "never mind" the next day. The seller can only cross that buyer's name off the list and drop down to the next highest bidder.

Buyers should not regard their bids as life-or-death decisions.

Buyers should read the pricing section of this book (pages 67–84). It will explain how the seller arrived at the price listed in the ad. Buyers must make a similar pricing evaluation to decide what they are willing to pay for this home.

Buyers have less time to make their decisions, however, and may find themselves in the middle of a bidding frenzy. Buyers should spend a little time defining their bidding strategy. They should bid only as much as they think the home is worth. When they reach the highest amount they are prepared to bid, they should stop.

The seller has not qualified any of the bidders. The top bidder may not be able to get a mortgage or may not buy the home for some other reason. The deal may fall through, and lower bidders may get a call weeks or months later, offering the home at the lower price. If this happens, it will probably be a very good deal for the buyer.

BIDDING STRATEGY

Let's say you've responded to an ad for a home selling for $99,500 or best offer. You've looked at enough homes to know this is as nice as others that have just come on the market asking $125,000. And this home is as appealing as those that have been on the market for six or nine months with a price dropped to $115,000.

You know that any price under $110,000 is a great deal for the home, and that a price between $110,000 and $115,000 is a good deal for the home.

You know the seller will get several bids under $99,500 from "undertakers" hoping the home will go very cheap, but there are too many knowledgeable buyers looking at the home for that to happen. The home will probably sell for somewhere between $99,500 and $115,000. It could sell for more if someone really wants this particular home.

The seller has told every potential buyer that the first bid in the round robin will go to the highest bidder prior to the end of the inspection. The second bid will go to the next highest bidder, and so forth. Bids must be separated by $500.

You are the first family to inspect the home. You are ready to buy. You want this home if you can get it at a good price. What should you bid?

There is a huge advantage to being the first bidder in round-robin bidding. The more bidders, the greater the advantage. You want to be the first bidder in the final bidding process, and you should place your initial bid to ensure that you will get the first bid in the round robin.

Your initial bid should be around $105,000.

A bid over the asking price tells the seller you are a serious buyer. Your bid announces to other buyers that no one is going to "steal" this home. Anyone else who wants this home is going to have to fight for it. You may be able to scare off other buyers who otherwise might think they have a chance.

You should call the seller before the inspection process is over to find out what the highest bid is. If the high bid is greater than yours, but less than what you are prepared to pay for the home, you should raise your bid so that you will be the first one called in the round robin.

Testing Thresholds

Sellers price their homes at price points. Buyers should regard these same price points as thresholds to be tested. For this home, thresholds come every $5,000: $100,000, $105,000, $110,000, and so on. Other buyers will set an upper limit at these numbers.

You should always take a position $500 above a threshold.

Spending $500 above an arbitrary threshold is not significant on a purchase price in excess of $100,000 that you plan to finance over a 30-year period. It will cost you less than $4 a month.

By positioning yourself $500 over a threshold, you force the next bidder to consider a price $1,000 over the threshold. The third bidder will have to consider a price $1,500 over the threshold. And so on. By the time the bidding returns to you, it will be approaching the next threshold.

If you still want the home, you would be wise to jump $500 over the next threshold.

If you're serious about buying the home, you must show other bidders that you are willing to bid at or above thresholds.

You will pay less for the home if you test other buyers than if you allow them to test you.

The strategy behind bidding is to always have the strongest bidding position. Then, even if someone else makes a higher bid, you wind up exactly where you want to be. You have the right bid in your own mind. If the home sells for the price you are willing to pay, you will own it.

Once you've bid on enough homes, you will eventually own a home you want, at a price you like.

PREEMPTIVE BIDDING

Some homes may be worth much more to you than to anyone else. Maybe the location is perfect, or it reminds you of something dear to you.

If you really want to buy a certain home, you should consider making pre-emptive bids. These bids jump two or more thresholds above the last bid. They tell all other bidders that you intend to buy this home, no matter what it costs, and that they will not be able to outbid you.

Preemptive bidding is designed to stop the bidding process, which is exactly what you want it to do.

Other bidders can then make their final bids at levels that are comfortable for them, under your bid, and wait to see if you are able to close the home at the price you have bid.

NOT JUST HOMES

The 5-Day Plan is not limited to home sales. Since I placed the original ad for my home, I've sold cars and boats, rented apartments, conducted tag sales and bartered household items using the same basic system.

I've used this strategy because it's fun, it's fast, and I can make more money than with any other approach. I've taught my children to sell things this way.

Smaller items take less time to sell—just Saturday and Sunday, in the typical case. If you put the item on the market any earlier, you'll only be overwhelmed by phone calls earlier. It will raise your advertising cost without yielding a higher price for the item. It's not worth it.

All the principles that apply to selling your home also apply to selling smaller items. The price listed in the ad is still the key factor. It must be low enough to attract a large number of buyers. If enough people bid, you'll get a fair market price for whatever you're selling.

You pick your advertising media the same way, except that a regional newspaper isn't necessary. For small items a single ad in the best local newspapers is usually sufficient. People won't come from far away to make a small purchase.

If you've done it properly, you'll still get as many as 100 calls over the weekend. The buyer pool is much larger for less costly items, and many people scour the classifieds for interesting deals. Yours should be the most interesting for that weekend, so you should get a lot of calls.

The system will work for any item if you follow all the steps:

- Write the rules.

- Talk to people on the telephone.

- Read from a script.

- Keep a log.

- Disclose everything.

- Explain the bidding process.

- Allow an inspection period.

- Conduct the bidding.

- Conclude the sale.

- Drop to the next bidder if the top bidder fails to show up immediately with cash in hand.

My son sold a 1984 Toyota Corolla Diesel with no engine using the 2-Day Plan. Before he ran the ad, the best deal he had was from a junkyard that offered to tow the car away if he paid them $50.

He disclosed everything in the ad and offered the car for $50 or best offer. Two days and 100 phone calls later, he was one happy fellow with $414.25 in his pocket after paying $10.75 for the ad.

Now people in my family routinely sell things by modifying the basic 5-Day Plan to fit the items they want to get rid of. We do it to liven up dull weekends. It's exciting—like gambling, except that you always win.

APPENDIX

I. PRICING WORKSHEET

You will find that establishing a price for the ad is the hardest and most time-consuming aspect of the sale. The process is not complicated. The calculations are not difficult. But there is no exact formula to follow, and ultimately you must make a judgment call about what price to list.

You must not price your home so low that you get too many potential buyers. You must not price your home so high that you get too few potential buyers. You must never lose sight of the fact that the offering price is not the selling price.

Still, you have to put something in the ad. Use the Pricing Worksheet on the following pages to figure it out.

PRICING WORKSHEET

Establish Price Points

1. What is the *most* you would *pay* for your home? $ _____

2. What is the *least* you would *take* for your home? $ _____

3. If line 2 is greater than line 1, you will have trouble selling your home.

Determine the Ballpark Price

4. Multiply line 2 times .9 $ _____

Find a Magic Number

5. If line 4 is just below a magic number, use it.

6. If line 4 is above a magic number, drop below the next lowest magic number.

7. Your magic number is $ _____

Test for Lowest Common Denominator

8. Look for other homes like yours. Your price must be at least 10% below any other listed price. If it is not, change it to a magic number at least 10% under any other listed price for a similar home.

9. Your lowest common denominator is $ _____

(continued)

Test on Friends and Family

10. Ask friends and family if they would buy your home for the price on line 9. Everyone should say yes without hesitation. If reasonable people who know your home do not jump at this price, keep lowering to a new magic number until everyone agrees that it is a great price.

11. Price everyone agrees is great $ _____

Test Yourself

12. If 40 buyers come to your home, and the best offer is 90% of the price on line 11, will you take it? If the answer is yes, the amount on line 11 is the price for your ad. If the answer to question 12 is no, insert the next highest magic number on line 7 and answer questions 8 through 11 again based on the higher number.

13. Continue testing yourself until you arrive at a price on line 11 that everyone agrees is great and that you are prepared to take 90% of. That is the price for your ad.

II. SAMPLE MATERIALS

The materials included in this section are samples of the information sheets discussed on pages 99–112. They should provide you with a useful format that you can adapt to specific information pertaining to the sale of your home.

You'll need about 100 copies each of the separate topics. Each topic should be printed on different-colored paper.

Note that an address and phone number appear at the top of each sheet. Buyers will be looking at many homes, and you want to be sure they don't confuse yours with any others they might be considering.

Remember, you can always stress the good points about your home when you speak to the buyers in person. But try to make each of your information sheets as detailed as possible in case you're too busy to spend much time in conversation during the inspection.

1829 LONG POND ROAD
(608) 555-3138

QUICK DESCRIPTION

Our home is a 5-bedroom raised colonial on a pond. It was built in 1965.

It has a dining room, kitchen, den with fireplace, 2 bedrooms, 3 baths, deck and patio, all overlooking the pond. Three bedrooms, a large living room and a 2-car garage face away from the pond.

The house has 2-zone oil baseboard heat, storm windows throughout, a full attic and plenty of closet space.

The overall size, including the garage, is approximately 3,000 sq. ft.

The property is within walking distance of schools and shops in central North Anytown.

The fair market value, assessed as of 10/1/92 by the North Anytown Tax Department, is $120,000. Our total yearly property tax is currently $2,200.

We purchased this home in 1987 for $152,500.

It sits on a 1-acre lot.

It will be open for inspection between 10 A.M. and 5 P.M. on Saturday and Sunday.

To get here, take Route 75 to Exit 35. Travel 1/2 mile north on Long Pond Road to No. 1829.

The home will be sold to the highest bidder on Sunday night.

1829 LONG POND ROAD
(608) 555-3138

DETAILED DESCRIPTION

Style:	raised ranch
Construction:	wood frame
Type of Roof:	gable
Roof Material:	asphalt
Chimney:	brick
Gutters:	aluminum
Windows:	wood frame, single-pane, double-hung
Storms/Screens:	aluminum
Siding Material:	wood shingle
Electrical Method:	100 amps /110/220 volts/copper wiring/circuit breakers
Heating:	oil/hot water /2-zone/ buried fuel tank
Water Heater:	"instant hot water"—no tank coil—oil
Water Supply:	submersible pump and well
Waste Method:	septic
Living Room:	32 × 15
Kitchen:	16 × 15	overlooking pond
GE 21-ft Side by Side Refrigerator
GE dishwasher
Magic Chef Double Wall Oven
Jenn Air Grill

Dining Room:	16 × 15	overlooking pond
Master Bedroom:	15 × 15	double doors/large bathroom
Bedroom 2:	12 × 11	overlooking pond
Bedroom 3:	12 × 11	overlooking pond
Upstairs Bathroom:	15 × 10	double sink

(continued)

Den:	23 × 15	overlooking pond
		fireplace
		sliding doors exit to patio
Bedroom 4:	11 × 11	
Bedroom 5:	11 × 11	
Downstairs Bathroom:	15 × 10	
Laundry Room:	Maytag washer and dryer	
Garage:	25 × 30	(attached)

1829 LONG POND ROAD
(608) 555-3138

DIRECTIONS

HOME OPEN FOR INSPECTION
10 A.M.–5 P.M. Sat. and Sun.

QUICK:

Take Route 75 north to Exit 35—Long Pond Road. Go north to No. 1829.

DETAILED:

Take Route 75 to Exit 35—Long Pond Road.
Turn left at light at bottom of exit ramp.
   (Same turn whether coming from north or south.)
   (Do not pass shopping centers—wrong way.)
Pass gas station on right.
3/10 mile to traffic light.
Continue straight, bearing right on Long Pond Road.
2/10 mile from light to 1829 Long Pond Road.
   (1/2 mile from Route 75 to 1829)
Mailbox numbers are clear from 1801 through 1829 on right side of road.
1827 and 1829 share same driveway.
1829 is home in back.
Gray home with white trim.
White mailbox.

(continued)

**1829 LONG POND ROAD
(608) 555-3138**

DISCLOSURE STATEMENT

The following disclosure statement is made to the best of our knowledge. It is not a warranty or guaranty of any kind. It is offered solely to help you evaluate this property. After the round-robin bidding, but before the closing, the high bidders will want to have this property examined by professional inspectors of their choice.

GENERAL INFORMATION:

Date Built: 1965
Date Purchased: 1987
Currently occupied by owners.
No additions, remodels or structural changes have been made since the house was built. The neighborhood is stable, and we are aware of no proposed changes.

PROPERTY:

See copy of survey for details.
The pond is a wetlands area and cannot be developed.
We have had no problems with drainage or flooding since we have lived here.
We know of no fill on the property.
We know of no earth-settling problems either on the property or in the neighborhood.
There are no boundary-line disputes or easements affecting the property.

(continued)

There are no existing or threatened legal actions concerning this property.

The property is not located in an earthquake zone.

We know of no toxic substances present on the property.

The property has been tested for radon. See copy of report.

We have never had a problem with termites, dry rot or pests.

STRUCTURAL ISSUES:

We are aware of no cracks or flaws in the walls or foundation.

We have had no problem with water leakage.

We have had no problems with the driveway, walkways, patio or garage.

We have removed the deck leading to the back door. It must be replaced at the new owner's cost. (Bid on the property as is— no deck!)

HOUSE:

See the Detailed Description sheet for specific information about the house.

All items mentioned in the Detailed Description are included in the sale.

The roof and rain gutters were replaced eight years ago. They have never leaked.

BID ON THE PROPERTY AS IS!

You will have time after the bidding to confirm all representations in this disclosure statement.

1829 LONG POND ROAD
(608) 555-3138

RADON REPORT

U.S. RADON SERVICES

January 6, 1993

Location: 1829 Long Pond Road, North Anytown, USA

Canister I.D. Number: 0251151

Start Time: 14:20

Start Date: 12/20/92

Stop Time: 16:00

Stop Date: 12/26/92

Analysis Time: 10:31

Analysis Date: 01/06/92

Your Radon Concentration is 1.1 pCi/L.

Follow-up measures at this level are probably not required.

The Environmental Protection Agency (EPA) guideline considers 4.0 picocuries (pCi/L) the "action level" for indoor radon; a level at which you should take steps to reduce radon in your home.

(U.S. Radon Services is an Independent Laboratory with no affiliation to the United States Government)

**1829 LONG POND ROAD
(608) 555-3138**

BIDDING METHOD

The home will be sold to the highest bidder in round-robin bidding Sunday night after the inspection is over.

The bidding will be open. I will tell anyone the status of the bids at any time.

Bids may be left at any time.

The highest bidder prior to the round-robin bidding will have the opportunity to make the first bid when the final bidding begins. The next-highest bidder will get the second call, and so on down the list.

Every interested bidder will have the opportunity to top the high bid until the highest bid is established.

If there is more than one bid at the same level, the earliest bid will be honored.

Bids must be $500 apart ($99,500/$100,000/$100,500, etc.).

I will call any bidder who wants to bid on Sunday evening, starting at 8:00 P.M.

The highest bidder will be offered the home at the bid price. If the highest bidder is unable to purchase the home, the second-highest bidder will be called. If this bidder is unable to purchase the home, the third-highest bidder will be called.

Bid on the home *as is*.

**1829 LONG POND ROAD
(608) 555-3138**

MORTGAGE TABLE*

MONTHLY AND TOTAL MORTGAGE PAYMENT COMPARISONS

Rate	Mortgage Amount	$99,500	$100,000	$100,500	$101,000	$101,500	$102,000	$102,500
7.00	Monthly	661.98	665.30	668.63	671.95	675.28	678.61	681.93
	Total Cost	238,312.80	239,508.00	240,706.80	241,902.00	243,100.80	244,299.60	245,494.80
7.25	Monthly	678.77	682.18	685.59	689.00	692.41	695.82	699.23
	Total Cost	244,357.20	245,584.80	246,812.40	248,040.00	249,267.60	250,495.20	251,722.80
7.50	Monthly	695.72	699.21	702.71	706.21	709.70	713.20	716.69
	Total Cost	250,459.20	251,715.60	252,975.60	254,235.60	255,492.00	256,752.00	258,008.40
7.75	Monthly	712.83	716.41	720.00	723.58	727.16	730.74	734.32
	Total Cost	256,618.80	257,907.60	259,200.00	260,488.80	261,777.60	263,066.40	264,355.20
8.00	Monthly	730.10	733.76	737.43	741.10	744.77	748.44	752.11
	Total Cost	262,836.00	264,153.60	265,474.80	266,796.00	268,117.20	269,438.40	270,759.60
8.25	Monthly	747.51	751.27	755.02	758.78	762.54	766.29	770.05
	Total Cost	269,103.60	270,457.20	271,807.20	273,160.80	274,514.40	275,864.40	277,218.00
8.50	Monthly	765.07	768.91	772.76	776.60	780.45	784.29	788.14
	Total Cost	275,425.20	276,807.60	278,193.60	279,576.00	280,962.00	282,344.40	283,730.40

*This table is believed to be accurate. However, neither the author nor the publisher can take responsibility for any errors or omissions.

(continued)

MONTHLY AND TOTAL MORTGAGE PAYMENT COMPARISONS *(continued)*

Rate	Mortgage Amount	$99,500	$100,000	$100,500	$101,000	$101,500	$102,000	$102,500
8.75	Monthly	782.77	786.70	790.63	794.57	798.50	802.43	806.37
	Total Cost	281,797.20	283,212.00	284,626.80	286,045.20	287,460.00	288,874.80	290,293.20
9.00	Monthly	800.60	804.62	808.64	812.67	816.69	820.71	824.74
	Total Cost	288,216.00	289,663.20	291,110.40	292,561.20	294,008.40	295,455.60	296,906.40
9.25	Monthly	818.56	822.68	826.79	830.90	835.02	839.13	843.24
	Total Cost	294,681.60	296,164.80	297,644.40	299,124.00	300,607.20	302,086.80	303,566.40
9.50	Monthly	836.65	840.85	845.06	849.26	853.47	857.67	861.87
	Total Cost	301,194.00	302,706.00	304,221.60	305,733.60	307,249.20	308,761.20	310,273.20
9.75	Monthly	854.86	859.16	863.45	867.75	872.04	876.34	880.63
	Total Cost	307,749.60	309,297.60	310,842.00	312,390.00	313,934.40	315,482.40	317,026.80
10.00	Monthly	873.18	877.57	881.96	886.35	890.74	895.12	899.51
	Total Cost	314,344.80	315,925.20	317,505.60	319,086.00	320,666.40	322,243.20	323,823.60
10.25	Monthly	891.62	896.10	900.58	905.06	909.54	914.02	918.50
	Total Cost	320,983.20	322,596.00	324,208.80	325,821.60	327,434.40	329,047.20	330,660.00
10.50	Monthly	910.17	914.74	919.31	923.89	928.46	933.03	937.61
	Total Cost	327,661.20	329,306.40	330,951.60	332,600.40	334,245.60	335,890.80	337,539.60

III. TELEPHONE LOG

Keep a copy of the phone log, together with the rest of your information materials, next to each phone in your home.

Along with the caller's name and phone number, write down any relevant information or impressions about the caller in the space provided. Be sure the person who takes the call signs the log.

Stress the importance of the phone log to all family members and friends who will answer the phone during the 5 days of your sale.

TELEPHONE LOG

Page _____

_____ (___) ___ - _____

_____

_____

_____

Taken by: _____

_____ (___) ___ - _____

_____

_____

_____

Taken by: _____

_____ (___) ___ - _____

_____

_____

_____

Taken by: _____

Page _____

_____ (___) ___ - _____

Taken by:

_____ (___) ___ - _____

Taken by:

_____ (___) ___ - _____

Taken by:

_____ (___) ___ - _____

Taken by:

IV. INITIAL BIDDING SHEETS

The forms on the following pages can be copied or kept in this book as a record of bids from prospective buyers.

Some reminders:

1. Bids must be $500 apart ($95,500/$100,000/$100,500, etc.).

2. If there is more than one bid at the same level, the earliest bid will be honored.

3. Be sure to get each bidder's telephone number.

4. Tell each bidder at what time the round-robin bidding will begin on Sunday night.

INITIAL BIDDING SHEETS

Bidder's Name	Telephone Number	Amount Bid
_____	(___) ___-___	$ _____
_____	(___) ___-___	$ _____
_____	(___) ___-___	$ _____
_____	(___) ___-___	$ _____
_____	(___) ___-___	$ _____
_____	(___) ___-___	$ _____
_____	(___) ___-___	$ _____
_____	(___) ___-___	$ _____
_____	(___) ___-___	$ _____
_____	(___) ___-___	$ _____
_____	(___) ___-___	$ _____
_____	(___) ___-___	$ _____
_____	(___) ___-___	$ _____
_____	(___) ___-___	$ _____
_____	(___) ___-___	$ _____
_____	(___) ___-___	$ _____
_____	(___) ___-___	$ _____
_____	(___) ___-___	$ _____

Bidder's Name	Telephone Number	Amount Bid
_____	(____) ____ - ____	$ _____
_____	(____) ____ - ____	$ _____
_____	(____) ____ - ____	$ _____
_____	(____) ____ - ____	$ _____
_____	(____) ____ - ____	$ _____
_____	(____) ____ - ____	$ _____
_____	(____) ____ - ____	$ _____
_____	(____) ____ - ____	$ _____
_____	(____) ____ - ____	$ _____
_____	(____) ____ - ____	$ _____
_____	(____) ____ - ____	$ _____
_____	(____) ____ - ____	$ _____
_____	(____) ____ - ____	$ _____
_____	(____) ____ - ____	$ _____
_____	(____) ____ - ____	$ _____
_____	(____) ____ - ____	$ _____
_____	(____) ____ - ____	$ _____
_____	(____) ____ - ____	$ _____
_____	(____) ____ - ____	$ _____
_____	(____) ____ - ____	$ _____
_____	(____) ____ - ____	$ _____

V. ROUND-ROBIN BIDDING SHEETS

After the last buyer has left on Sunday evening, transfer all your notes and records from your telephone log(s) and Initial Bidding Sheets to the Round-Robin Bidding Sheets that follow.

Make sure you have contacted every potential bidder and you know everyone's bid prior to the start of the round-robin bidding.

The sheet should be set up with the highest bidder first, then the second bidder, and so on.

Write in both the first and last names of the bidders, their phone numbers and the amount of their bids. If a couple has bid together, you should have the names of both individuals even if they say only one of them will be doing all the bidding.

Start the bidding exactly when you told all bidders you would start. Read the terms at the top of the first Round-Robin Bidding Sheet. There is nothing special about the terms I've listed. They were my terms. Yours may be different.

Just be sure you read the same terms to every bidder.

ROUND-ROBIN BIDDING SHEETS

Read to each bidder:

"I will call all interested bidders until there is one high bid, and no other bidder wishes to top it. All bids must be at least $500 apart. If there is more than one bid at the same level, the earliest bid will be honored first.

"If the top bidder is unable to purchase the home, the next bidder will be called. If that bidder is unable to purchase, the next bidder will be called. The three top bidders will be offered the house.

"Currently the high bid is $_____. Do you want to advance the bid?"

Number	Name	Telephone Number	Bid
1. _____		_____	$_____
_____		_____	$_____
_____		_____	$_____
_____		_____	$_____
$_____	$_____	$_____	$_____
2. _____		_____	$_____
_____		_____	$_____
_____		_____	$_____
_____		_____	$_____
$_____	$_____	$_____	$_____

Number	Name	Telephone Number	Bid
3. _____		_____	$_____
_____		_____	$_____
_____		_____	$_____
_____		_____	$_____
$_____	$_____	$_____	$_____
4. _____		_____	$_____
_____		_____	$_____
_____		_____	$_____
_____		_____	$_____
$_____	$_____	$_____	$_____
5. _____		_____	$_____
_____		_____	$_____
_____		_____	$_____
_____		_____	$_____
$_____	$_____	$_____	$_____

Number	Name	Telephone Number	Bid
6.	_____	_____	$_____
	_____	_____	$_____
	_____	_____	$_____
	_____	_____	$_____
	$_____ $_____	$_____	$_____

Number	Name	Telephone Number	Bid
7.	_____	_____	$_____
	_____	_____	$_____
	_____	_____	$_____
	_____	_____	$_____
	$_____ $_____	$_____	$_____

Number	Name	Telephone Number	Bid
8.	_____	_____	$_____
	_____	_____	$_____
	_____	_____	$_____
	_____	_____	$_____
	$_____ $_____	$_____	$_____

Number	Name	Telephone Number	Bid
9. _____	_____	$_____
_____	_____	$_____
_____	_____	$_____
_____	_____	$_____
$_____ $_____	$_____	$_____

10. _____	_____	$_____
_____	_____	$_____
_____	_____	$_____
_____	_____	$_____
$_____ $_____	$_____	$_____

11. _____	_____	$_____
_____	_____	$_____
_____	_____	$_____
_____	_____	$_____
$_____ $_____	$_____	$_____

Number	Name	Telephone Number	Bid
12.	_____	_____	$_____
	_____	_____	$_____
	_____	_____	$_____
	_____	_____	$_____
	$_____	$_____	$_____ $_____

13.	_____	_____	$_____
	_____	_____	$_____
	_____	_____	$_____
	_____	_____	$_____
	$_____	$_____	$_____ $_____

14.	_____	_____	$_____
	_____	_____	$_____
	_____	_____	$_____
	_____	_____	$_____
	$_____	$_____	$_____ $_____

CHECKLIST

CHECKLIST

		See Pages
☐	1. Be sure you're really ready to sell your home.	45
☐	2. Decide when you want to sell it.	57–66
☐	3. Line up an attorney.	191–92
☐	4. Have your home inspected.	87–88
☐	5. Test for radon.	87
☐	6. Price your home.	69–84
☐	7. Figure out what to fix. Fix it......................	89–96
☐	8. Write your ad.	115–122
☐	9. Decide where to place your ad.	123–24
☐	10. Decide on your rules of sale.	105
☐	11. Make copies of materials for your sale.	99–112
☐	12. Set up a telephone log.	133–34
☐	13. Review with your family what everyone's role will be; line up friends if you need them.	135
☐	14. Review your ad. Place it.	115–24
☐	15. Did you do it right?	125–26
☐	16. Receive calls from prospective buyers; enter names and notes in log	137–38
☐	17. Clean your home.	143–44

(continued)

		See Pages
___	18. Set up security.	145
___	19. Make "open house" signs.	147–48
___	20. Lay out your materials.	153
___	21. Set up your "office."	155
___	22. Set up bidding sheets.	246
___	23. Put up explanatory signs if necessary	157
___	24. Welcome prospective buyers to your home.	159–60
___	25. Show your home; sort out buyers	163–73
___	26. Review bidding procedure with buyers; enter bids on bidding sheets.	177–86
___	27. Call your bidders exactly when you told them you'd call; conduct the round-robin bidding.	187–88
___	28. Give all information about the sale to your attorney.	193–94
___	29. Review the contract with your attorney. Sign the contract.	195–96
___	30. Close the sale of your home.	197–98